Writing That Means Business

Also by Ellen Roddick:

Holding Patterns
Together
Young Filmmakers

Ellen Roddick

Writing That Means Business

How to get your message across simply and effectively

Collier Books
MACMILLAN PUBLISHING COMPANY
New York

MACMILLAN PUBLISHING COMPANY
866 Third Avenue, New York, N.Y. 10022
Collier Macmillan Canada, Inc.

Library of Congress Cataloging-in-Publication Data

Roddick, Ellen
  Writing that means business.

  Bibliography: p.
  Includes index.
  1. Business report writing. 2. Commercial correspon-
dence. 3. Memorandums. 4. English language—Business
English. I. Title.
HF5719.R63   1986   808'.066651   85-32578
ISBN 0-02-015380-5 (pbk.)

First Collier Books edition 1986
10 9 8 7 6 5 4 3 2 1

Printed in the United States of America

*Macmillan books are available at special discounts
for bulk purchases for sales promotions, premiums,
fund-raising, or educational use. For details, contact:*

Special Sales Director
Macmillan Publishing Company
866 Third Avenue
New York, N.Y. 10022

Writing That Means Business is also published in a hardcover edition by
Macmillan Publishing Company.

Contents

Acknowledgments

My special thanks for sharing with me their thoughts on the state of writing in business today go to—

David Brown, motion picture producer (*Jaws, The Sting, The Verdict*, and other films)

Helen Gurley Brown, author and *Cosmopolitan* editor in chief

James F. Campbell, former ambassador to the Republic of El Salvador

Leo Cherne, executive director, The Research Institute of America

Arthur N. Coleridge, former manager, Book Department, Readers Digest Association, London

Richard E. Deems, former chairman, Hearst Magazines

Wallace W. Elton, senior vice president, International Executive Service Corps

William M. Fine, president, Dan River Mills

William Gofen, Gofen and Glossberg

Geraldine Henze, director of Communications Programming, Graduate School of Business, Columbia University

J. K. Jamieson, former chief executive officer and chairman,
    Exxon Corporation
Gordon Jones, vice president, The Hearst Corporation
Robert W. Lear, former chief executive officer and chairman,
    F. & M. Shaefer Corporation
Lois Lindauer, international director, The Diet Workshop
Richard J. Lord, president, Lord, Geller, Federico, Einstein
John T. Morris, president, Edgewater Steel Company
Harrison A. Roddick, former partner, McKinsey & Company
Jerry I. Speyer, managing partner, Tishman Speyer Properties
Digby Whitman, writer and consulting editor

Introduction

For most people in offices, hard copy is the only evidence of ever having done anything. Unless you can be measured directly by profit-and-loss standards, what else do you have to show for all those days in the office?

> Geraldine Henze
> Director of Communications Programming
> Graduate School of Business
> Columbia University

T his book is designed to help you improve your writing. Language is a tool. Properly handled, it enables you to communicate your ideas to readers without significant loss of meaning or intention during transmission.

Clear and persuasive letters, memos, and reports will make a good impression on your business associates. If you increase the effectiveness of your writing, you will sharpen your competitive edge.

Colleagues—both inside and outside your organization—may form their impressions of you solely or primarily from what you write. Senior management, for instance, increases its familiarity with middle management in this way. Senior executives prefer writing from subordinates that does not have to be rewritten.

Alfred Sloan, the legendary chief executive officer of General Motors, provides an example of how business acumen may be enhanced by strong, convincing writing. Early in his career at GM, he wrote "Organization Study," a memo describing his ideas about decentralization as the key to success for the company. The memo ultimately convinced the board of directors that Sloan could run GM— which he did with great success as CEO from 1923 to 1946.

The General Electric Company's leaflet, *Why Study English*,* states:

> Every day in your future you will be called upon to speak and write, and when you open your mouth or write a letter or report, you will be advertising your progress and your potential worth.

Not all self-advertising is positive. To illustrate what can happen when managers write thoughtlessly, here are some derailed idioms and metaphors that have been taken from actual business communications.

---

* As quoted in Courtland L. Bovee, *Business Writing Workshop* (San Diego, Calif.: Roxbury Publishing Co., 1980), p. 58.

It's mañana from heaven.

He makes reports with the seat of his pants.

We're not giving up by any shake of the imagination.

That's driving her up a skull.

The softening of orders has finally come to roost.

He really lowered the timber on him.

Look into this in a much closer vein.

Insurance rates are dropping like flies.

Don't run off at the handle like a stuck cow.

We'll really have to polish the lily.

They're chewing the breeze.

It stood out like a bell.

We've got to keep our ear to the wheel on this one.

The new product crept sideways into the marketplace.

Let's not jump before the cart here.

She'll give you some background and histrionics on the subject.

Two-family houses are hotter than sliced bread.

We're head over heels over the competition.

On the pages that follow you will find a variety of techniques for writing effectively.

THE EFFECTIVE WRITER

Strives for	*Shuns*
Accuracy	Abstraction
Balance	Ambiguity
Brevity	Anger
Cogency	Apology
Confidence	Clichés
Conviction	Confusion
Courtesy	Digression

Strives for	*Shuns*
Directness	Disclaimers
Forcefulness	Dishonesty
Humaneness	Error
Incisiveness	Evasion
Interest	Exaggeration
Logic	Gruffness
Lucidity	Hypocrisy
Moderation	Indecision
Order	Jargon
Persuasiveness	Obsequiousness
Precision	Pretension
Rapport	Redundancy
Relevance	Sexism
Simplicity	Stiffness
Sincerity	Timidity
Specificity	Vagueness
Thoroughness	Verbosity

Think Before You Write

Last week when I was in Tucson, the man I was meeting with made one after another of those diagrams as we talked. I had no idea what he was doing. The next time we meet, I'll be making them, too!

> *Participant in a Roddick Communications seminar for fast-track managers, after being introduced to the free-form diagram*

Organizing ideas in a horizontal outline rather than in the traditional, vertical outline liberates me.

> *Robert C. Rugen*
> *Vice President*
> *Employee Relations*
> *Pitney Bowes*

H ave you ever heard anyone admit that he or she hates to think? People are more apt to say they hate to write. Oddly, in business it often does not occur to us to think before we write. We plunge in, constructing sentences and paragraphs. This does not necessarily get results. Is there a better way? Yes. Organize ideas by jotting them down, using only a few key words, before you begin to write—in other words, diagram.

We will explore two kinds of diagrams—the free-form diagram and the tree diagram. These are not the diagrams of sentences that you may have made in grade school. Instead, they are maps of your thoughts and ideas.

What Are Diagrams?

Diagraming provides crucial advantages
Diagrams are visual organizers that allow you to get all your ideas down as they occur to you. In a linear (traditional) outline, you have to wait until an idea is relevant before you include it—and by then you may have forgotten it. A diagram is so flexible that it grows as you think, and you don't have to worry about how an idea fits in—that comes later (after you've committed all your ideas to paper).

Diagraming uses more of your mind than outlining does
You may be wondering why, if diagraming is such a great idea, it hasn't been common practice in business for years.

The answer is simple. Current techniques for diagraming are based on new discoveries about how our brains function. Old-fashioned techniques for making linear notes or outlines draw mainly on our brain's linear capacity for processing information sequentially, one unit at a time (envision a digital watch, which shows only the present hour and minute).

Now we know that our brain can also process many pieces of information simultaneously, forming whole patterns in a flash (envision an analog watch, which shows all 12 hours and all 60 minutes at once). By diagraming our ideas, we draw on both aspects of our own brainpower.

Many people already use diagrams

As a communications consultant with my own firm, Roddick Communications Ltd., I have discovered through working with clients that the results of diagraming are very practical:

- A manager in a Fortune 500 company explained his problem with writing on the job by saying, "I write one paragraph, and it's not clear, so I write another paragraph, and that's not clear either. Then I write a third unclear paragraph. And I end up with three pages that my boss tells me to clarify and reduce to one page." Since he learned to diagram his ideas before writing a single sentence, he can write that one clear page.
- Two participants in a seminar for technical people found that by diagraming ideas before writing, they accomplish in forty minutes what previously took two hours.
- A public relations consultant, who dictates rather than writes, was criticized for correspondence that sounded too much like rambling conversation. She discovered that she can dictate cohesively and persuasively by diagraming what she wants to say, then dictating from that.

Free-Form Diagrams

What is a free-form diagram and when do you use it?

When you're trying to make sense out of a large or confusing mass of information, you can get a handle on what you want to say by starting with a free-form diagram. A free-form diagram is a variation on the "mind maps" developed by Tony Buzan in England and described in his book, *Use Both Sides of Your Brain.* On pages 12-13 of this book there is a free-form diagram that summarizes the major features of composition in writing for business. It is a diagram of the contents of this book—an overview in diagram form— and could serve as a starting point for writing the book.

A free-form diagram resembles the cross-section of a tree as seen from a bird's-eye view above. Remember, no two trees are ever identical—and the same is true of free-form diagrams (in fact, you might think of them as tree-form diagrams).

You can make a free-form diagram

In making a free-form diagram, you write only *key words*, and you turn your paper (which should be at least as large as a sheet of typing paper) sideways. A pencil and eraser are the tools of choice, as they allow you to change your mind easily.

How to Make a Free-Form Diagram

1. Draw a central circle (like a crosscut of a tree trunk). In this circle write a description of why you

are writing. Try to use the infinitive form of a verb —for instance, *To propose new warehouse;* or *To recommend split shifts for working mothers;* or *To report on meeting with client.* Or use a question that this communication must answer.

2. Draw a branch out from the trunk for each main idea you want to include; write the idea down on that branch-line, using a few key words. Do not try to arrange ideas in any particular order.

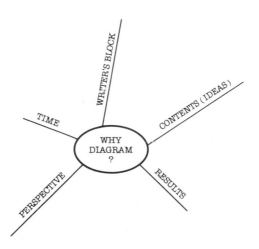

3. Draw a twig whenever you think of an idea related to one of the ideas you have placed on a branch (or on another twig). Attach each twig to a branch or to another twig, and write a few key words on it. You need not draw all the twigs that belong on one branch before drawing the next branch. And you need not draw all the branches before drawing twigs. Work spontaneously.

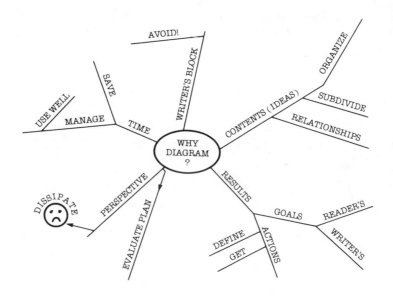

4. Add each idea as it occurs to you, in whatever position strikes you as appropriate. Group the most important ideas around the center and work out to the periphery, where minor points show up.
5. You are not bound by the tree analogy. Some artistically inclined business people use dotted lines, arrows, and small sketches to represent and connect ideas. Embellish your diagrams as the impulse strikes you.

Work as fast as you can, and don't edit your ideas or your language. Later, any idea in the diagram can become the center of another diagram, if you wish—just as the center of the diagram on page 11 comes from the periphery of the free-form diagram on pages 12-13. Your object is to draw a picture of your ideas about the topic. If you include irrelevant ideas or attach subpoints to inappropriate major points or end up with a key topic on a twig

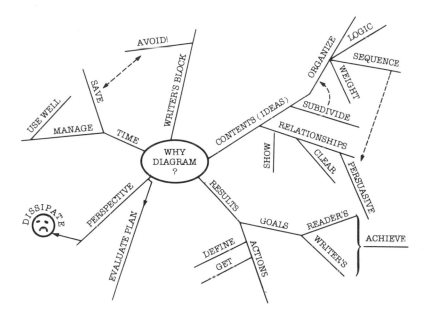

instead of on a branch, don't fret. Diagram, tear up, and discard as many times as necessary to arrive at an effective presentation of your thoughts. Your time is worth more than your scratch paper.

You can write or dictate directly from a free-form diagram. Free-form diagrams are a form of mind map, and Peter Russell wrote *The Brain Book*, which is over 200 pages long, using "a set of 7 major mind maps, springing from which came some 150 minor maps. . . . It was only when the book was finally being prepared for printing that it was transposed into linear form."

Free-form Diagram

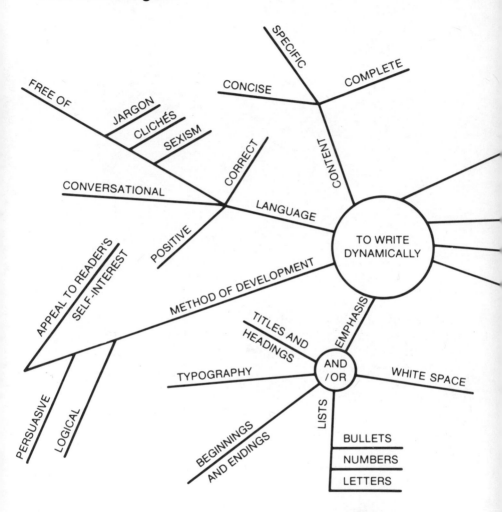

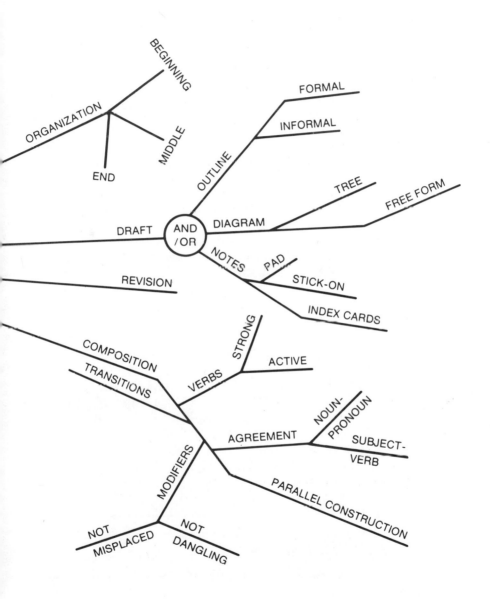

Tree Diagrams

What is a tree diagram and when do you use it?

The tree diagram is useful for organizing information logically. Like free-form diagrams, tree diagrams help you to get down on paper everything you want to include. In addition, they provide a form for arranging ideas in convincing order, without wasting time writing sentences or paragraphs in the preliminary stage. Some business writers transfer ideas mapped out on a free-form diagram to the more logical tree diagram.

While a free-form diagram suggests a tree seen from above, a tree diagram resembles a chart. It may remind you, in fact, of a genealogical chart. Or you may associate it with a flow chart; feel free, if you do, to improvise and create a flow chart of what you want to write. On pages 16–17 of this book there is a tree diagram that summarizes the order in which business letters, memos, and reports should be organized. By following this diagram, you could write directions for how to organize business writing.

The tree diagram is based on the decision tree, which was originated by, among others, Howard Raiffa, a founder of the field of decision analysis who has developed "techniques to help decision makers think more systematically about complex choice problems," according to the Harvard Business School.

You can make a tree diagram

Turn your paper horizontally when you make a tree diagram. In this position, it has several names—a decision tree, an analysis tree, an organization tree, a horizontal outline, or a Harvard outline. When you turn your paper vertically and work your tree diagram from top to bottom, it is called a pyramid diagram. Whichever way you turn your paper, use a pencil and a good eraser.

How to Make a Tree Diagram

1. At the far left, state your subject. Try to use an infinitive form of a verb—*To sell marketing plan.* Or ask a question that your communication must answer.
2. On the branches to the right of your subject, describe in a few key words your major points or topics. The diagram on pages 16–17 has three branches in this position *(Beginning, Middle,* and *End).* But you may draw as few as two or as many as seven (people have trouble remembering more than seven chunks of information at a time).
3. Place subordinate points and subtopics, using key words to indicate your ideas, on branches to the right of the assertions they support.

At the start, you don't need to insert ideas into the diagram in a convincing order. Later, number them in their final order (and so avoid copying the diagram). By the time your diagram is complete, be sure that the ideas branching from a premise are similar in nature— e.g., questions, steps, criteria, reasons; they should relate clearly and consistently to one another and to the idea they support.

If you are using visual aids—charts, graphs, tables, maps—attach the branches representing them to the branches representing the points they support. Draw branches indicating visual aids, however, in a different color of ink from the ones you are using to map the text.

16

Tree Diagram

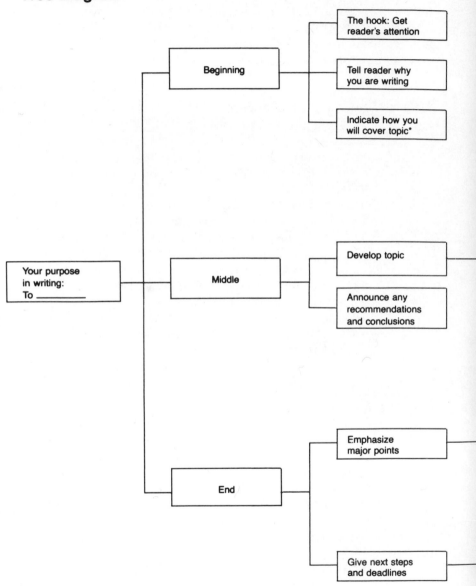

* If you are writing at length

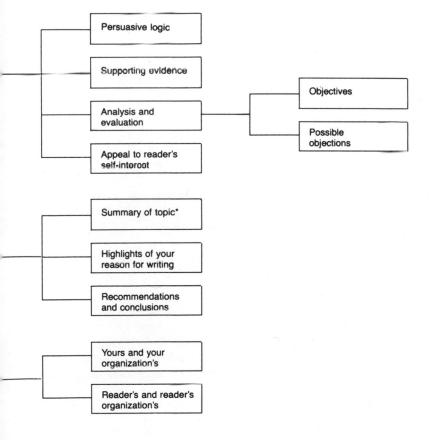

Or go over with a colored highlighter the branches and key words that indicate use of a visual.

The importance of generalizations

Although you may have heard, in other contexts, that generalizations are bad, in organizing writing for business, generalizations are good. In the diagram—

The highest level of generalization is your subject statement at the far left.

The branches immediately to its right hold the next highest level of generalization, e.g., in the tree diagram, *Beginning*, *Middle*, and *End*. If you are diagraming a report, you can draw headings from this level.

The specific details that support your generalizations branch to the right on the page.

When you use the tree diagram to organize a report, create a separate diagram for each section. People who outline long reports sometimes transfer the formal outline to a series of tree diagrams. Then they line up the tree diagrams under each other. Looking down the line of diagrams, they can tell whether their ideas are presented logically and consistently—and whether all the points in a vertical row are at the same level of generalization.

Stick-on notes and an artist's pad

While designing a tree diagram, you may discard several pieces of paper and write each idea several times (as you cross out, rearrange, and start anew). If you prefer to write ideas only once, use stick-on notes. Write each idea on a separate note. Then stick the notes down in a tree-diagram pattern. You can move your ideas around repeatedly without having to rewrite.

Use a different color of paper for each level of generalization to color-code your ideas according to the weight you give them. For instance, the first row of ideas on the left will be yellow; the row to its right will be blue; and the next row to the right will be green. If you're using visuals, indicate them with smaller, white notes.

Have you ever noticed someone at a meeting writing on stick-on notes and sticking them on a large artist's pad resting in her or his lap? One scientist who was doing this explained when asked, "No speaker organizes his thoughts well enough to suit me. So I write down his best points on stick-on notes, then organize them on the pad. I rearrange them as he talks. If he says something halfway through that closely relates to the idea he opened with, I just stick the new point near the opening idea on the pad. By the end of the speech, I have a tightly organized summary of what I've heard."

Members of many different professions are beginning to pick up this technique and are diagraming reports—before beginning to write—by using stick-on notes on artist's pads.

Summing Up

Free-form diagrams and tree diagrams are visual organizers that can help you in your career by saving time and producing results.

Because people balk at the unfamiliar and resist changing comfortable habits, however, you probably will have to make a conscious effort to learn and adopt new diagraming techniques. If you do work at them for a couple of weeks, until they become familiar, you will give yourself a chance to spend less time writing and enjoy writing more. Diagraming will then pay off as a valuable professional skill.

Communicating Without Static

If business people (in our business, account executives) could only learn to write as they speak in an honest, open conversation, all our communications would be the better for it.

> Richard J. Lord
> President
> Lord, Geller, Federico, Einstein

If it is just one page, I promise to read it with attention. If it is longer, my secretary will put it straight into a wastepaper basket.

> *Attributed to Winston Churchill*

L etters, memos, and reports should communicate to the reader in a direct and accessible way. Too often, correspondence and reports are created more for the writer than for the reader—and when this happens, the written message becomes counterproductive and self-defeating.

This chapter covers ten aspects of skillfully written letters, memos, and reports.

The Ten C's

Effective writing is not a mysterious, hit-or-miss affair. In business, good writing is—

1. Clear
2. Candid
3. Concise
4. Correct
5. Coherent
6. Complete
7. Concrete
8. Convincing
9. Constructive
10. Conversational

1. Be clear

Lucid paragraphs composed of explicit sentences should make your reason for writing obvious to your reader.

Don't leave any doubt in your reader's mind about

your exact meaning. Sentences like these, if read literally, may be both unintentionally amusing and confusing:

No: The new director of public relations worked her way up from the reception desk to her present high office.

Yes: The new director of public relations started her career as a receptionist.

No: There isn't any question about the proposed advertising campaign's success in the opinion of the account executive.

Yes: The account executive believes that the proposed advertising campaign will succeed.

No: Before we can send up our satellite, it must be fully covered with insurance.

Yes: Before we can send up our satellite, we must insure it fully.

Readers appreciate a straightforward approach. Say simply what you have to say, and then stop. Avoid jargon, buzz words, and paralegal or bureaucratic phrases.

Jargon	*Translation*
To adjudicate	To judge
Caveat	Warning
De facto	Really
Economically disadvantaged	Poor
To enjoin	To order
Feedback	Response
To dollarize	To compute the cost
At this point in time	Now
Impacted	Affected
Matrix	Context, variety

Jargon	*Translation*
Parameters	Limits
Prima facie	Apparently true
To procure	To get
Qua	As
To quantify	To reduce to numbers
Quasi	Almost
Riffed	Fired
Subsector	Portion

While writers hope that jargon sounds impressively technical and shrewd, many readers react to it with distaste. Obscure, pretentious, trendy language is the foe of intelligibility—a smoke screen designed to disguise murky thinking and personal insecurity.

No: Here's a decent option, because it impacts excellently on our viable interface with labor, and that's the bottom line.

Yes: This is a good choice because it supports our sound relations with labor, and that's essential.

Where you need a technical word—like *matrix* or *prima facie*—and your reader is not likely to understand it, define the term the first time you use it. Also define acronyms and abbreviations when you first use them.

Watch out for homonyms. They are words with the same spellings or pronunciations but with different meanings. Used near each other, they may slow down a reader.

No: Before he *tabled* the motion, he referred to the *table* on page six of the report that had been placed on the *table* in front of him.

Yes: Before he *tabled* the motion, he referred to the *chart* on page six of the report that had been placed in front of him.

Certain kinds of words give our language structure. They tend to remain unchanged over time and are the scaffolding upon which are hung the words whose meanings shift and evolve. As long as the structure words fall into place, a sentence will sound more or less reasonable, even if it is nonsense.

Structure words are italicized in these two examples, one sensible, one not.

> *The four* division heads *are* meeting *in the* library *because it is the* quietest room.
>
> *The four* minduson fobs *are* dilling *in the* brantoly *because it is the* kenlex hoad.

Choose with special attention to meaning the words that fall between the structure words. Avoid weakening a sentence by burdening it with more structure words than it needs.

2. Be candid

Tell your readers the truth and nothing but the truth. They know when you're trying to disguise bad news or inflate good news. Exaggeration creates doubt; so do euphemisms.

Anyone who is recognized as having deceived, misled, or lied to colleagues is suspect forever.

Don't fudge on unfavorable information. Say you don't know if you don't know. Where doubt prevails, acknowledge doubt.

3. Be concise

Mark Twain is supposed to have said that he didn't write *metropolis* because he was paid the same amount for writing *city*. Today he might be paid more for writing *city*, if he were writing in business, where brevity is appreciated.

Don't let sentences and paragraphs run on—and on—and don't use a long word where a short one will do as well.

Don't repeat what your reader has written to you. Instead, start right in and answer the memo or letter. If you must refer to it, do so succinctly.

No: This is in reference to your memo of November first regarding use of the company dining room for personal entertaining.

Yes: Your question about use of the company dining room touches upon a current policy dispute.

By saying only what needs to be said and using only the words needed to say it, you will steer clear of—

- Digressions
- Redundancies
- Irrelevant details
- Stating the obvious

Prune your prose. Excesses of language that are common in business communications include—

Overdone	*Improved*
Advance planning	Planning
Advance warning	Warning
Ask the question	Ask
A small number of	A few
At a later date	Later
At a time when	When
Basic fundamentals	Basics
Brief in duration	Brief
Due to the fact that	Because
Endorse on the back	Endorse
General public	Public
In view of the fact that	Because
Merged together	Merged

Overdone	Improved
Mutual cooperation	Cooperation
Not in a position to	Can't
Regular monthly meetings	Monthly meetings
Remains still	Remains
Repeat again	Repeat
The color brown	Brown
The reason is because	Because
Time of day	Time
Without further delay	Immediately

Unrestrained use of adjectives and adverbs dilutes your writing. Choose them carefully.

Diluted

She is a *very good* technician, who works *efficiently* and *imaginatively*.

Direct

She is an *efficient* technician, who works *imaginatively*.

4. Be correct

Have all your facts, figures, and dates right. Be fussy about spelling, grammar, and punctuation. Address the appropriate people, accurately spelling their names and using their titles. The very people whom you most want to impress are often the ones who will zero in on errors.

Be precise in your use of words. Some typical errors made in business are corrected here:

Don't write	When you mean
~~Adjure~~ _implore_	Abjure _to abstain from_
Administrate	Administer
Affect _influence_	Effect _result_
Alternate	Alternative
Bona fides	[*Bona fide has no plural*]

Don't write	*When you mean*
Comprised	Composed
Data is	Data are *or* Datum is
Different than	Different from
Disinterested	Uninterested *or* Indifferent
Economical	Economic
E.g.	I.e.
Equable	Equitable
Etc.	Et al.
- Farther	Further
Hopefully	I hope that
I'll call you	Good-bye
Infer	Imply
Invaluable	Valueless
Maybe	No
Media is	Media are
Mitigate	Militate
Transpire	Occur

(handwritten marginal notes: "uniforra, even" beside Equable; "distance" beside Farther; "in addition, moreover" beside Further; "To be used as a conclusion" beside Infer; "suggest" beside Imply; "to have weight or effect" beside Militate)

5. Be coherent

Support major points with concrete ideas that relate unambiguously to them. Connect ideas to one another in ways that will make obvious sense to the reader.

Don't confuse the issue with extraneous information.

Provide only relevant data and documentation.

Limit communications to one primary topic. Where you deal with several major aspects of your topic, divide your argument into as many sections.

Come to the point. Don't explain first. Explain second.

No: We've run out of stock unexpectedly. I won't bore you with the details. Needless to say, we are desperate and hope you will fill the attached order at once.

Yes: Please rush the attached order through as fast as you can. We've run out of stock unexpectedly and need new supplies at once.

6. Be complete

Give readers all the details they need. Include deadlines, pertinent resources, contacts, criteria, and alternatives. Supply definitions and explanations where they will illuminate.

Assess your reader's level of expertise, and insert suitable background material.

If related information is available elsewhere, tell your reader where to find it.

Enlist anecdotes, quotations, and particular examples when they help to make a point.

7. Be concrete

Generalizations should be used judiciously and supported with reliable evidence. Be as specific as possible, even where this entails writing at greater length:

No: Nature's Best health food for dogs had a good year.

Yes: Last year, sales of Nature's Best health food for dogs increased 60 percent, and distribution went up 44 percent.

No: We have been able to attract many outstanding artists to our stage.

Yes: Here are the names of one hundred outstanding artists who have appeared on our stage over the past five years.

No: The general feeling around here is that the mall will never be built.

Yes: A majority of the town board is on record as being against the mall.

Tell readers what you expect from them and when; tell them what you will do and when:

No: Please let me know your answer soon.

Yes: Please let me know your answer before February third, when I leave for our sales conference.

Prefer direct statements to abstractions:

Weak
    Honesty is one of her virtues.

Stronger
    I have never heard her lie.

Strongest
    She never lies.

8. Be convincing

Keep your message sincere and plausible. Don't embroider or distort. Cite authorities when you can. Demonstrate that you've done the research. Explore pros and cons.

Often, to write simply is to write forcefully. Listen to what you write.

Wordy and weak	*Simple and stronger*
Move forward	Advance *feminize*
Rich businesswoman	Tycoon
Afford an opportunity	Give a chance
Terminate	End
In a position to	May, can
Inquire	Ask

Clichés are ineffective because they have been heard so often that they have become stale. For example—

Tired executive
Limp handshake
My case rests
Richly deserved
Bright idea
Lost in thought
Separate the men from the boys*

Sports metaphors are so popular in business that even though they are clichés, they are an exception to the rule. You're more likely, nevertheless, to hear colleagues use phrases like these in conversation than to see the phrases in writing:

Par for the course
Shoot from the hip
A good track record
Tackle the problem
Not a three-inning player
They've used all their time-outs
Jump the gun
A grandstand play
Hit the track running
Out in left field
The ball's in your court

Qualifiers limit your responsibility, and this evasion irritates readers. Be careful not to create doubt in the reader's mind with such wishy-washy words and phrases as—

We trust that you
If you wish
It is our hope that
Should you want us to
It seems to me

---

* Separate the women from the girls, on the other hand, is still fresh.

> Perhaps
> Apparently
> As a rule
> Normally

Shirking responsibility by throwing in disclaimer clauses does not win readers' respect, either.

No: We forecast economic recovery early next year unless unforeseeable international events have adverse effects here at home.

No: We expect to sponsor your television series as long as its content—which we would not try to influence in any way—continues to be in line with our goals.

9. Be constructive

Diplomatically avoid words and phrases that make readers defensive. For example—

> Unreasonable
> Misinformed
> Questionable
> Overreaction
> One-sided
> Rejection
> Unfortunately
> The blame, error, failure, fault
> You claim, allege, maintain
> You neglected, overlooked, forgot
> I insist, require, demand, must repeat
> I cannot comprehend, believe, permit

Allow readers to save face, regardless of the righteousness of your position. Offer readers alternatives. Grant them the benefit of the doubt. Make room for them to compromise or to come around to your side.

Compliment your reader whenever you can do so sincerely. Cultivate generosity of spirit and a supportive attitude in your writing.

Shun bigotry, sexism, narrow-mindedness, and rigidity.

If you're giving a reader both good and bad news, concentrate on the positive:

Negative

Health and performance problems associated with executive stress escalate wherever a corporation fails to provide a supportive environment.

Positive

Executives under stress perform better and are healthier in corporations that provide a supportive environment than in those that do not.

Negative

Dependence on a management information system (MIS) specialist undermines a senior manager's power by denying her or him direct access to information.

Positive

A senior manager who has direct access to the management information system has more power than if she or he is dependent on an MIS specialist.

Whenever possible, take a positive approach:

Negative

You won't be sorry that you chose our firm.

Positive

You'll be glad that you chose our firm.

Negative

I can't see you until I finish this report.

Positive
   I'll see you as soon as I finish this report.

10. Be conversational

The best writing strikes a conversational tone but avoids the digressions and hesitations of speech. Writing is better organized and more specific than talk.

   If you want to write as unaffectedly as you speak, try reading aloud what you've written and then rewriting any sentences that sound stiff and awkward.

   Although dictation is indeed spoken, not everyone has a knack for talking with the orderliness, brevity, polished grammar, and vigor required when words meet paper. That's why so many careful writers in business—whether they write or dictate—edit and revise their work.

   Naturalness is superior to stuffiness, and gobbledygook befuddles the mind:

Nonsense	*Sense*
Authoritative feedback is deficient.	No one knows.
Personnel's tolerance of a transitional framework is negative.	People resist change.
Construct an optimal manipulative strategy.	Make it work.
There's been a breakthrough in top-level ideological polarization.	The board of directors has finally reached a compromise.

   Don't try to attain an ideal norm. Relax. Speak in your own voice. Let your own personality shine through your words. Gradually, your own style develops, and it's the best style for you.

Use the same vocabulary you use in conversation: don't adopt a pompous, stilted, formal vocabulary for writing.

Adapt your tone to the situation.

Summing Up

Good writing in business carries a direct and precise message to the reader. The best writing is, therefore, clear, candid, concise, correct, coherent, complete, concrete, convincing, constructive, and conversational.

3

Letters and Memos That Engage Readers

*In business communications, verbosity, sloppi-
ness, and intellectual laziness are the cardinal
sins.*

> *John T. Morris*
> *President*
> *Edgewater Steel Company*

*Business writing should define the problem and
suggest a commonsense solution with a course of
action.*

> *Richard E. Deems*
> *Former Chairman*
> *Hearst Magazines*

G uidelines are given here for writing letters and memos that are effective with readers. Observations about form are followed by a section on substance outlining seven familiar kinds of correspondence.

***

Form

***

The Address

Be a perfectionist. When you write an address, see that it's complete and correct. Include your return address.

The Date

If your organization has a modern image, favor the streamlined date style that is advocated by the University of Chicago Press: The date is given before the month, and there are no commas.

1 April 1984

If, however, your organization has a conservative, traditional image, stick with the good, old-fashioned style:

April 1, 1984

Filing Instructions

Include filing instructions where they are acceptable. They immediately draw the reader's attention to your central idea and later insure quick access from the files.

When you use a title line, it serves as filing instructions. Skip the salutation on a memo, if you wish, but always give a memo an underlined title. Make the title direct and informative. Never sacrifice meaning to brevity.

No: Enhancement of office park grounds

Yes: Your proposal to stock the pond near the parking lot with bass

The Salutation and the Sign-off

Address a memo only to the person or people you expect to take action based on the information it contains. Send copies to people you simply wish to keep informed. When a memo goes to several people, list their names in alphabetical order or—if distinctions of rank are indisputably clear—in order of importance.

Choose the salutation and the sign-off thoughtfully. Motion picture producer David Brown has this to say—

> The salutation has to be carefully measured. *Dear David* suggests something routine. *My dear David* suggests something very serious and perhaps ominous. *Dearest David* is intimate. *Dear Brown* is probably from some WASP friend.
>
> I sign a letter *Warm regards* or *Affectionately. Love,* if I mean *love.*

How you address your reader depends on your relationship. If you're on a first-name basis, use the first name; if you're not, don't. Decide whether or not to substitute the more informal comma for the businesslike colon.

Dear Burton:
Dear Burt,

If you've met the reader but don't know her or him well—or if you know each other only by reputation or through mutual acquaintances—consider using both first and last names in the salutation. This practice may be more readily accepted at higher than at lower levels of management.

Dear Terry Greene:

When you write to someone with a title, use it, and use it correctly. To banish doubt, consult a list of forms of address.* If, for instance, you're writing to the attorney general of the United States, do not use a name in the salutation. Instead, pick one of these.

Dear Mr. Attorney General:
Dear Madam Attorney General:
Dear Sir:
Dear Madam:

Here are some commonly accepted sign-offs:

Sincerely,
Sincerely yours,
Cordially,
Cordially yours,
Warmly,
Regards,
Best regards,
Very best regards,
My best wishes,
All the best,

When you've written an unpleasant letter, don't sign it with warmth and cordiality. Limit yourself to sincerity.

No: We felt obliged to tell your prospective employer that we consider you a bad risk.

Warmest good wishes,

* See "Helpful Books," pp. 112–113.

Do you prefer changing with the times to preserving tradition? Are you at ease placing the day before the month or including both first and last names in a salutation? Then you probably won't hesitate to streamline the sign-off: Place your signature flush with the lefthand margin, and eliminate the complimentary closing. In any case, don't allow your signature to slant down from left to right— readers tend to interpret a down-slanting signature as a sign of pessimism or lack of confidence.

If your name does not reveal your gender, include in the typed signature on letters to people who don't know you, *Mr., Ms., Miss,* or *Mrs.* If your name is ambiguous and is on the letterhead but isn't typed, then write in the form of address. This is also a good way for a woman to let the reader know how she wants to be addressed.

Blake Robart

Ms. Blake Robart

The Message

An inter- or extra-office memo is usually more direct and less formal than a letter.

How a memo is organized should be apparent at a glance. You may send a memo in outline form or with lettered or numbered points. For longer memos, an introductory summary, a closing recapitulation, and various kinds of emphasis create an obvious order. Always keep your readers in mind and write specifically for them.

The ease with which memos are written and distributed leads many writers to produce a blizzard of unnecessary correspondence. Moreover, as Lois Lindauer, international director of The Diet Workshop, says—

> There is a certain point at which memoranda become part of a distancing process. The more memoranda between people, the more distance is created. This situation, in turn, promotes less effective management and motivation.

Limiting memoranda to a single thought or request makes it easy to keep track of what's alive in the copy. After that issue has been dealt with, the memo can be tossed or filed.

When you write letters, remember that they have, if only obliquely, the potential to contribute to your organization's financial health. It pays, then, to pay close attention to letter writing. How is your reader significant to your firm? Keep the answer in mind as you write.

Managers who use word processors for correspondence need to be especially watchful. Don't let the fact that you *can* fix errors "easily—later" satisfy you; that fact is relevant only if you *do* fix errors. Readers see what is sent, not what might have been sent.

Long and complex letters require tight reasoning and an orderly presentation of ideas. Short, informal messages lend themselves—perhaps—to more casual reasoning and presentation, but remember that *brevity is the soul of wit.* Readers want to know as quickly and easily as possible what you have to say.

The Conclusion

It is neither necessary nor desirable to close with sweet nothings. As soon as you've completed your message, cease writing and sign off, rejecting such banalities as—

I hope this has answered all your questions.

Please call me if we can be of further help.

We trust this matter will receive your careful attention.

If you do want something—such as a firm decision within ten days—say so specifically. Restate in conclusion the action you wish taken and the date by which you expect the reader to act. Be explicit about what your own actions will be and when they will occur.

A personal note at the end of a letter or memo to someone with whom you are on friendly terms adds warmth. Refer, for instance, to the reader's family, to a sport he or she enjoys, or to the last time you saw each other.

Substance

Here are tips on writing seven familiar kinds of communications:

1. Information or acceptance

In this most routine of letters, announce your subject, expand on it, and close—leaving the reader with a sound understanding of why you wrote.

Camilla dear,

Fantasima's new designs are brilliant. I saw them yesterday.

At last, jewelry so obviously fake that the wearer need not risk mugging and mayhem to appear in it, yet so ravishingly imaginative that collectors will spring up everywhere.

The new designs are perfect for your editorial pages. Do hasten to the showroom—and behold the fantasy.

I'm eager to hear what you think, as soon as you've had a look.

Warmly,

Trudy

Gertrude Marlene Todd

2. Sales or persuasion

Dramatic flair yields dividends here. Grab the reader's attention with a distinctive opening. Marshal facts that prove the desirability of the product, service, or idea you offer. Appeal to the reader's emotions. Then close assertively, because you want the reader to act at once—before interest fades.

Dear Arlene,

Your restless, knowing customers demand new kicks constantly, *n'est-ce pas?* With our latest designs, you can offer them a rush that won't quit, that's both legal and safe.

Fantasima's latest necklaces, bracelets, and earrings promise sensuous pleasure and aesthetic pride—at prices that discourage satiety. Boswick Gibbs and NATALIE both used our pieces in the presentations of their new lines last week, and the media (as you doubtless noticed) cheered us—along with them.

The messenger who delivered this letter—and a token sample (nonreturnable) of what Fantasima has to offer—awaits your notation on the attached card of the date and hour when Andrew and I may expect your visit.

Cordially,

Sam

Samantha T. Beatty

3. Request

Don't be defensive and apologize, explain, or declare gratitude before you announce what you're after. Disclose right away what it is you want. Remind your reader, in a light tone, about anything you've done for her or him recently.

If circumstances warrant, explain why you want whatever you want. Close pleasantly, with appreciation for the co-operation you trust will be forthcoming.

Dear Jacques,

The next time you're up at *Chic*, would you show them those smashing pictures that you took of Fantasima's current designs on the afternoon when you were testing your new lens?

We were flattered when you borrowed an eclectic assortment of our pieces to use at your shooting the next day. Sam hopes you'll include the best of those shots, too.

You understand what a boost it will give Sam and me if Fantasima gets into the magazine. *Chic* readers are exactly the customers who will embrace us.

Your help at this critical point in our careers will be genuinely appreciated and long remembered by Samantha and by me.

Best regards,

andy

Andrew Adler

4. Complaint

No whining. No ranting. You need the reader's assistance. Give a complete description of the problem. Provide all details the reader needs to make amends. Be explicit about what you expect the reader to do. Include the date by which you require a response. If previous correspondence hasn't got results, tell what you'll do if the situation is not corrected immediately. As a last resort, write to the president of the organization. If the organization is responsible to a regulatory body, report the problem to the regulatory group, and send a copy to the organization's president.

Check bounced by bank's error
Fantasima account, #72864319

    Our landlady reports that you returned our rent check (#1653) and claimed that Fantasima had insufficient funds to cover it. Nonsense. We had, in fact, more than enough in the Fantasima account to cover the rent on our office.

    Three weeks ago we deposited a check for $4,000, drawn on another of your branches. According to the money machine in your lobby, that amount has never been credited to our account.

    We told our landlady to redeposit our rent check. We expect you to honor it and, in addition, to write apologies this week to us and to her, explaining the bank's error.

    A copy of her letter to us is attached to this letter, as is a copy of our deposit slip.

Andrew Adler

Andrew Adler

5. Rejection

Because it's unpleasant to turn someone down, to disappoint, to refuse a request—writers of negative letters often follow a natural inclination to hide behind formal language and stuffy sentiments. Be brave, be decent: write rejections that cushion the reader. Keep your language friendly and conversational. Design an opening that prepares the reader for bad news. Then deliver the bad news directly but gently. Explain tactfully why you are saying *no*. If you can leave open any doors to the future, so much the better.

Dear Mr. Grigio:
    Your array of feathers sounds gorgeous. Mr. Adler and I can imagine feathers being used—by the right designer— to create spectacular jewelry.

We, however, would not be comfortable working with feathers (we're both vegetarians), so we can't give you an order. Fantasima never features shells, horn, or any other material that comes from animals, fish, or birds.

If you expand your line to include semiprecious stones or materials made by people, please come see us with those.

Regards,

Samantha T. Beatty

Ms Samantha T. Beatty

6. Collection

It's in your best interests to approach the reader courteously as well as firmly. A debt overdue by many months demands a more forceful confrontation than a payment overdue by but a single month. Threaten only those actions you are prepared to take. Suggest ways the reader can help to resolve any disagreement between you about the debt. Enclose a return envelope.

Dear Ralph:

Has there been some misunderstanding? Surely, you don't believe Fantasima let you have all those pieces on consignment? Yet we still haven't received your check for them. You did receive our bill?

Please be a steady chap and send us your check, in the enclosed return envelope.

As Samantha explained at the start, we cannot extend credit. You're automatically charged interest on payments overdue by more than thirty days.

If there has been a mixup, and you have a cancelled check covering the order, do send us photocopies of both the back and the front of it.

We're proud to place Fantasima in your celebrated boutique, and we look forward to having this matter cleared up, so we can continue to enjoy the prestige and pleasure of doing business with you.

Sincerely,

Andrew

Andrew Adler

7. Goodwill

These letters may be short and are often handwritten. They inform, invite, support, sympathize, thank, or praise. They speak to the reader as a human (not exclusively as a business associate). The fact that letters of goodwill need not necessarily be written makes them all the more effective.

Summing Up

Use the correct forms for correspondence. Pick a suitable salutation and sign-off. Design the message to be as easy as possible for the reader to understand. Conclude without banalities.

In this review of seven familiar types of correspondence, **B** = Beginning; **M** = Middle; **E** = End:

1. *Information or acceptance*
   B —State the topic.
   M—Discuss or explain it.
   E —Conclude; summarize; reiterate your expectations.

2. *Sales or persuasion*
   B —Capture your reader's attention with idea or offer.
   M—Bombard reader with convincing facts, emotional appeals.
   E —Urge reader to act (or to agree) immediately.

3. *Request*
   B —Disclose what you want, and remind reader of any recent favor you've done for her or him.
   M—Describe, where appropriate, why you want what you want.
   E —Affirm your gratitude for the help you hope to get.

4. *Complaint*
   B —Announce what's wrong.
   M—Provide details enabling reader to help.
   E —Declare what you expect reader to do next.

5. *Rejection*
   B —Build bridge of sympathy to reader.
   M—Bury rejection in middle, justifying it while allowing reader to save face.
   E —Emphasize any positive aspects of situation.

6. *Collection*
   B —Present courteously the details of the overdue payment.
   M —Ask politely for immediate payment.
   E —Mention any action you plan if payment is not immediate. (Enclose return envelope.)
7. *Goodwill*
   B —Express thanks, praise, congratulations, or sympathy; extend an invitation.
   M —Support expression with personal details.
   E —Close with warmth.

4

How to Streamline Reports

Write plain, understandable English, as simply as possible.

> *James F. Campbell*
> *Former Ambassador to the*
> *Republic of El Salvador*

The commonest defect in business writing is simply that it lacks spark. I suspect this is largely because business writers think of themselves as just that— business *writers; instead of, as they should—* busi- ness *writers.*

> *Digby Whitman*
> *Writer and Consulting Editor*

W hat sort of report you have to write will influence how you rank and relate your ideas. Questions about sorting major and minor points are tied in here with decisions about structure and logic. The goal is to convey all the necessary information directly to readers without confusion or irrelevancies.

> # Kinds of Reports

There are four basic reports:

1. *Information*
   Provides information only; e.g., a historical report puts on record the history of a product, process, or event.
2. *Evaluation*
   Provides evaluation as well as information; e.g., a financial report assesses economic conditions.
3. *Conclusion*
   Provides conclusions as well as information and evaluation; e.g., an overview report discusses an entire business and is designed to minimize reader apprehension.
4. *Recommendation*
   Provides recommendations as well as information, conclusions, and evaluation; e.g., a planning report gets a business activity started or stopped.

Shaping a Report

You'll probably be working against a deadline when you write a report. Decide how much time the project merits, and resist waiting until the last minute to begin.

Resist, too, the temptation to look for guidance in the files. The fact that the reports you find there were approved does not, alas, guarantee their competence.

When your company uses a standard format, certain decisions about arrangement, composition, and length have been made for you. Readers, moreover, know what to expect. Without an official formula, you yourself are free to come up with a design that shows off your theme to best advantage.

Although some reports must be formal, a letter or memo form suits others. Whatever form you choose, doesn't it make sense to produce a first draft requiring a minimum of revision? The key to accomplishing this is acquiring adequate research notes and then arranging your ideas, based in part on those notes, skillfully.

To give shape to your ideas, start by grouping them, with a view to framing tight generalizations and supporting evidence. Diagram your ideas as described in Chapter 1. Use a tree diagram to—

- List your major ideas.
- Combine major ideas, where doing so raises them to a higher level of generalization.
- Distribute subordinate points beneath the ideas they corroborate.
- Clarify any obscure relationships among your ideas.
- Illuminate opaque connections and implications.

People remember best the ideas that are displayed in clear relationships. Each secondary idea must have an obvious connection to the main idea.

Readers aren't sponges, passively absorbing what they read. They read actively—judging, agreeing, disagreeing, interpreting, objecting, questioning. Write for an inquiring mind.

Don't tell readers how you reached your conclusions. They will be confused if asked to retrace your wandering steps with you. Assemble ideas in a meaningful pattern so that readers reach the same conclusions you've reached but take a more direct route.

Here are ten different ways to present information:

1. *Chronological*
   You're moving your stock from one warehouse to another. You outline the sequence of events in the order in which they will occur, and you give any firm dates.

2. *Geographical*
   There's been a population shift in the country. You discuss the effects of that on your business, area by area.

3. *Hierarchical*
   You're writing a succession study. Proceed from the candidates for chief executive officer to those for chief operating officer to potential department heads.

4. *Procedural*
   Your organization is upgrading its computer facility. You enumerate the successive steps to be taken.

5. *General to specific*
   You recommend entering the computer game market. You go from that generalization to an assessment of specific games you want your firm to produce.

6. *Specific to general*
   You've come upon a new product that seems right for your company. You work from a description of that

product to a description of the general requirements for your organization's developing, marketing, and selling it.

7. *Most to least important*
   You're adding a new flavor to your line of soups. You assess the sources of supplies, starting with the most crucial ingredient and working down the list.

8. *Least to most important*
   You have a public relations problem. You begin with the least alarming aspect of it and finally acknowledge that something serious may have occurred.

9. *Cause to effect*
   You've discovered a flaw in a supplier's copper tubing. You have to discuss the problems that have resulted from your company's use of that copper tubing.

10. *Effect to cause*
    Your atomic reactor has malfunctioned. You must explain what happened, beginning with the nuclear accident.

To organize a long report, sort ideas into clusters under six or seven generalizations. Raise generalizations to their highest levels. Some writers list generalizations as numbered points, while others prefer to use an outline form.

Diagraming your ideas before writing a first draft clarifies complex ideas. By comparing several sketchy diagrams that show the relationships between major and minor points, you're able to examine various plans for arranging your argument and then to choose the best. Use colored markers and highlighters to give proper weight to divergent elements and to show connections.

Decide whether your report will benefit from either deductive or inductive logic: *deductive reasoning* moves from the general to the specific and is by its nature sound; *inductive reasoning* moves from the specific to the general and may be sound or unsound. Deduction provides an air-tight argument but induction provides more interesting reading.

Deduction

Basis for conclusion
All A2Z computers use Ipswitch Basic. The Executive Micro is an A2Z computer.

Conclusion
Therefore the Executive Micro uses Ipswitch Basic.

Induction

Conclusion
Engineers are well-advised to become both managers and technicians because:

Basis for conclusion
A. Aeronautical, chemical, and electrical engineers have had to face, at various times recently, a softening job market in their respective fields.

B. With increasing frequency, companies seek engineers whose planning skills complement their technical skills.

C. Engineering schools have not been able to predict reliably, for entering students, which engineering specialists will be in demand when those students graduate.

Writing a Report

With your notes or outline—and perhaps a diagram—in hand, writing a first draft should be relatively painless. Flesh out your skeletal plan with muscular prose.

Writers who need to read and reread their words prefer typing, writing longhand, or using a word processor to dictating.

Write in the first person singular, unless your organization favors the first person plural. If you're writing for someone else, or if you're pulling together data that's already been interpreted by others, you may want to use the third person, or the pronoun *one*, or even the passive voice (which does not reveal the doer of the deed: *it was decided*).

New ideas may occur to you while you're working on your first draft. Fit them into your plan or diagram before you incorporate them into the text—to be certain the new ideas are relevant and are placed in positions of optimum strength.

Become your reader. Will the ideas that your reader receives be the same ideas that you think you're expressing?

This all-purpose organizational outline for a report is based on the suggestions of Harrison A. Roddick, a former partner of McKinsey & Company:

1. Introduction: state your subject and objectives.
2. Describe your methods and criteria.
3. List conclusions and recommendations.*
4. Present the facts and their sources, explaining facts' relevance.

* If these will upset reader, save them until the end.

5. Analyze and evaluate the facts, giving supporting evidence.
6. Draw tentative conclusions.
7. Suggest possible courses of action.
8. Evaluate each course of action in terms of objectives and in terms of potential objections.
9. Insert cost considerations, if applicable.
10. Give final conclusion.
11. Recommend a course of action in detail.
12. Conclusion: summarize report.
13. Include appendix if needed.

Whether or not your first draft is also your final version—as it may be for an informal report—edit and revise what you have written.

You have finished writing and revising a report when you can answer these questions affirmatively:

• In each section, will readers perceive one central theme?
• Is the central theme buttressed securely by subordinate ideas?
• Are subordinate ideas presented coherently and without irrelevancies?
• Is the point of view consistent?

Summing Up

Reports may be characterized by how far they go. The four basic kinds of reports give—

1. *Information*
2. *Information and evaluation*

3. *Information, evaluation, and conclusions*
4. *Information, evaluation, conclusions, and recommendations.*

The information within a report should be presented in a logical and appropriate order, with easily identifiable major points that are thoroughly supported by related ideas.

As the writer, sit in the reader's chair. Is the report you mean to write the same report the reader will read?

You and Your Reader

I almost never use the telephone. I put it in writing. It gives them a chance to think about it and gives me a chance to think about exactly what to say. And it's on record.

   Robert W. Lear
   Former Chief Executive Officer and Chairman
   F. & M. Shaefer Corporation

*Letter writing is not my normal mode of communication, as it is for my wife [*Cosmopolitan *editor, Helen Gurley Brown]. I mostly telephone, because I don't have the patience to write good long letters. Or good short letters. When I do write a letter, I take pains not to make it mundane or dull.*

   David Brown
   Motion Picture Producer
   (Jaws, The Sting, The Verdict, *and other films*)

This chapter recommends discretion in deciding whether or not to write at all. There are suggestions here for winning your reader's interest and sympathy, once you have decided to write. And, finally, there are sections about developing an appropriate tone of voice and a non-sexist vocabulary.

To Write or Not to Write— Perchance to Duplicate?

Too often, executives are asked to read useless documents. Office copying machines have triggered an epidemic of duplication, as letters, memos, and reports are distributed indiscriminately.

The manager who can be relied upon not to waste a reader's time with irrelevant material is likely to have her or his written words read promptly and attentively.

Before you write—and again before you duplicate—be sure the reader actually needs the information and needs it in writing.

Face-to-face conversations often take less time than does writing. So do telephone calls. Since the typical typed page is estimated to cost over $8, today, a long-distance phone call may be more economical than a letter.

QUESTIONS TO ASK YOURSELF BEFORE WRITING

- Is this information that cannot be conveyed adequately, appropriately, and effectively in conversation?
- Is a meeting a better idea than sending several copies?

- Is this information that should be on record or be available for reference?
- Is now the best time to make this communication?
- Is writing the most practical or the most diplomatic means of access to the intended reader?

The Reader's Point of View

A writer shows enlightened self-interest by concentrating on the reader. It is the reader, after all, and not the writer who is to be convinced, informed, appreciated, or spurred to action.

We are self-absorbed and are attracted to promotion of whatever we want.

Tell readers what your communication means to them. Being sensitive to their needs helps you approach readers positively. Be explicit about anything you want them to do.

Flatter your readers' intelligence, and don't explain words or points they can reasonably be expected to recognize, but tell them everything they need to know.

Be certain that you are addressing the right person. *Cosmopolitan* editor in chief, Helen Gurley Brown, observes in connection with advertisers that—

> There is a tendency to feel you must go to the top or you won't get proper attention. Going to the top is frequently the worst way to get your idea sold, because the decision will be made by somebody *underneath,* who will possibly be aggravated because he wasn't contacted in the first place. You just have to use a little judgment about whom to solicit.

Approaching the Reader

Demonstrate that it's in your reader's best interests to go along with you.

What's in it for her or him?

How is what you need compatible with what she or he needs?

Try to capture the attitude you'd take if your reader were sitting across from you and you were talking.

What do you hope he or she will think and feel about what you are saying?

What response do you hope to elicit?

Play a troubleshooting role.

Anticipate and answer questions and objections before they arise.

Make your meaning so unmistakable that your words cannot be twisted or misinterpreted and used against you by political adversaries.

Tighten your reasoning until it's more difficult to find flaws in your argument than to comply with your suggestions.

Make it hard for readers to say *no*.

Where you have had relevant conversations or correspondence with your primary reader, try to work in a reference to that when you write.

You and *your* can be more powerful words than *I* and

my (or *we* and *our*) when they're used to make a reader feel important. Insincere flattery and false modesty, however, are easily detected and undermine your position.

Keep an eye on the *I*'s in your writing; add *you*'s as often as you can. Move the spotlight from yourself to your reader. On the simplest level, for example—

Instead of

I need cooperation to make this work.

Write

Your cooperation can make this work.

The Elements of Style, by William Strunk, Jr., and E.B. White, cautions the writer to: "Sympathize with the reader's plight (most readers are in trouble about half the time)."

If you do this conscientiously, you are likely to—

- Be understood
- Not be misinterpreted

Where you are understood and are not misinterpreted, you avoid writing a clarification later and perhaps avoid more serious trouble as well.

There is a horribly extreme example in Harrison Salisbury's *Black Night, White Snow* of a memo that was misinterpreted.

Salisbury writes that Lenin once passed a note to a comrade at a meeting, asking how many counterrevolutionaries were in prison. The comrade jotted down, "Around 1,500," and passed back the slip. Lenin marked an *X* beside this reply and returned it. His comrade subsequently ordered all 1,500 prisoners shot. Lenin's secretary later explained that Lenin habitually marked an *X* beside a reply to show he'd read it. He had not wanted the prisoners shot.

Controlling Tone and Nuance

Hitting the right note means judging your message and your reader. Decide whether to be informal (but not offensively familiar); or to be formal (but not absurdly stuffy); or to chart a course between these poles.

Be conservative in your use of humor, which is difficult to put across in writing. Readers not only laugh at different things, but when they can't see your expression or hear your voice, they may misunderstand—and take offense at—what was intended as a friendly little joke. Even when the primary reader chuckles, the next reader will not necessarily be amused.

Proceed with caution, but do proceed. Humor can be invaluable in making a tough point. An amusing touch in correspondence or reports makes them entertaining to read as well as to write. In some offices, witty communications receive the swiftest attention.

Since tact and good manners are as important in business as elsewhere, anger, disparagement, accusations, and sarcasm seldom have a place in correspondence and reports; irony is rarely effective. A negative approach antagonizes most of us, making us uncooperative.

Writing a scathing letter filled with flare words and brilliant insults may be therapeutic. Sending it is a big mistake.

Be diplomatic.

Nonsexist Language

If *man* is a generic term, then why don't we feel comfortable with a sentence such as—

> Modern man no longer pampers himself during pregnancy. He leads an active life and often continues at his job right up to the day he goes into labor and gives birth.

In increasing numbers, women and men alike take umbrage at sexist language. But what responsible reader resents nonsexist language?

Casey Miller and Kate Swift, in *The Handbook of Nonsexist Writing,* provide page after page of suggestions (like the ones given below) for making language less discriminatory.

For	*Substitute*
Weatherman	Weather caster
Workmanlike	Skillful
Statesmanlike	Diplomatic
Fellowman	Fellow citizens, fellow humans
Workingman	Worker, wage earner
If a man can	If someone can
The man in the street	The person in the street
No man	No one
A man who lies often	A chronic liar
Mankind	Humankind
Man of letters	Distinguished writer
To man the pumps	To work the pumps
Manhours	Operator-hours, worker-hours

For	*Substitute*
Manmade	Synthetic
Manpower	Human power, muscle power, personnel
Manhandle	Mistreat
Male nurse	Nurse
Mailman	Mail carrier
Foreman, forelady	Supervisor
Layout man	Layout planner
Lady lawyer	Lawyer

According to that unimpeachable source, *The Oxford English Dictionary (OED)*, it is acceptable to use *they* or *their* for a single person whose sex is unknown to you, as in—

Will the *person* who returned my wallet please tell me who *they are* so I can thank *them?*

This usage will, nonetheless, offend purists who don't read the *OED*.

Other solutions to the problem of discriminatory language are to—

1. Substitute *you* or *one* for *she* or *he*.
2. Use both *she* or *her* and *he* or *his*.
3. Omit the pronoun.
4. Pluralize.

In other words—

Instead of
Every trainee wants to demonstrate *his* ability.

Write
As a trainee, *you* want to demonstrate ability.
As a trainee, *one* wants to demonstrate *one's* ability.

Every trainee wants to demonstrate *her or his* ability.
Every trainee wants to demonstrate ability.
Trainees want to demonstrate *their* abilities.

As for *Ms*, *Miss*, and *Mrs.*, it is courteous to follow the preference of the woman you're addressing. If you don't know her preference, use *Ms*, or omit a title but use both her first and last names.

Here are possible ways to write a salutation when you don't know the sex of the reader.

Instead of Sir *or* Madam, *write*
> Dear Sir/Ms
> Dear Madam or Sir

Or use a job title
> Dear Sales Manager
> To the Sales Manager
> Dear Commissioners
> To the Commissioners

Or use the company name
> Dear Southern Skies Airline
> To Southern Skies Airline

Or use a category
> Dear Sportsperson
> Dear New Car Owner

Any awkwardness about using a nonsexist vocabulary fades as new habits replace old prejudices.

Summing Up

Write only when there is no better way to communicate. And don't send unnecessary duplicates. Keep whatever you write as short as possible, and be sensitive to tone and nuance. Shun sexist language.

Always focus on the reader's viewpoint. You already know what you want to say. Be sure that your reader will know what you want to say, too. In business, writing for yourself instead of for your reader amounts to sabotage and is a perversion of the rules of communication.

Composing Your Ideas

State your purpose in the first paragraph. Don't try to trick me into the purpose, which is on page three.
> Gordon Jones
> Vice President
> The Hearst Corporation

In my very first sentence I must capture the attention of those I am addressing. In the first paragraph, I must state the essence of what I'm writing about. I must either be brief or be damned sure that what I have to write is sufficiently interesting to hold the reader's attention.
> Leo Cherne
> Executive Director
> The Research Institute of America

I n this chapter, methods are described to help you define your topic, shape your thoughts, and present your argument convincingly to your reader. There are also discussions of how to write commanding sentences and paragraphs and of how to use smooth transitions to keep the reader's mind moving right along with yours.

Organization

WHY MANAGERS WRITE:
To inform
To convince
To get action
To create goodwill
To appraise results

Writing and thinking are intimately connected. James O. McKinsey, founder of McKinsey & Company, is said to have emphasized to his staff that clarity in writing *forces* clarity in thinking; fuzzy and opaque writing betrays fuzzy and opaque thinking.

The first step in writing a letter, memo, or report is to decide what to include and what to omit.

If you are writing at someone else's request, don't hesitate to ask questions about the assignment. Find out everything you need to know about what is expected of you.

Do all the necessary research. Writers in business, many executives complain, fail to do their homework. Alden S. Wood, in his *Raglan Report* column, "The Typochondriac," advised dryly: "Do the work. Look things up. Be sure you're right. Amaze your readers."

There is no single correct way to design a theme. If the topic is simple, you may organize it in your head. With more complicated or lengthy material, you'll probably need to make preliminary notes, even if you eventually dictate.

WAYS TO PLAN WHAT TO SAY

- Diagram or outline your message.
- Jot down ideas, using three-by-five cards or a word processor; then arrange ideas logically.
- Make notes on a pad; underline and number major points.
- Think in terms of a beginning, a middle, and an end.
- Phrase the question this communication ought to answer.

According to Jerry I. Speyer, managing partner of Tishman Speyer Properties—

> Letters, memos, and reports present three major annoyances: lack of specificity, lack of clarity, and verbosity. In order to save time, people should use the five *W*'s to summarize their points.

THE FIVE *W*'s

Who
{
is the primary reader?
else will read this communication?
are you to the reader?
should perform specified actions?
}

What
{
is the scope of this communication?
do you hope to accomplish?
do you prefer to avoid?
criteria are you using?
is fact, what opinion?
is your solution or conclusion?
are the alternatives?
must be done to avert catastrophe?
are your real and seeming motives?
are the reader's real and acknowledged motives?
is the reader's response likely to be?
questions might the reader ask?
does the reader already know about this subject?
}

Why $\left\{\begin{array}{l}\text{are you writing to this particular person or group?}\\\text{are you writing now?}\\\text{have you reached your conclusion?}\\\text{are you issuing warnings?}\\\text{should the reader care about what you are saying?}\end{array}\right.$

Where $\left\{\begin{array}{l}\text{does this communication lead?}\\\text{does it fit into your relationship with the reader?}\\\text{are the reader's blind spots and biases?}\\\text{are the reader's points of resistance?}\end{array}\right.$

When $\left\{\begin{array}{l}\text{will additional information be available?}\\\text{will relevant actions and events ideally occur?}\\\text{are any deadlines involved?}\end{array}\right.$

It will help your reader to grasp and remember the contents of a complex letter, memo, or report, if you—

- *First*, tell briefly what subject you will treat and how you will treat it.
- *Second*, present your ideas one at a time, in an appropriate order.
- *Third*, review the highlights of the material you have presented, including any conclusions.

The recapitulation echoes but does not repeat the opening summary. For example—

Opening summary

   As you know, the lease on our New York office is running out. After studying alternative locations, we are convinced that we should move this division to Westchester. Factors leading to our conclusion outweigh significantly those militating against it: Positive and negative considerations are discussed below.

Middle

   [Here, the pros and cons of the move are explored.]

Recapitulation

We recommend moving this division to Westchester when the current lease expires early next year. In the long run, we will save money—despite the expenses of moving. Although a few of our people will have a much longer commute, they make up less than a third of our staff.

There are several reasons behind the recommendation to move. One is that our success does not depend on daily contact with colleagues in the city. Another is that we can benefit from Westchester's pool of mothers who prefer part-time to full-time jobs, since our planned diversification will create such positions. Most important, if our relocation succeeds, headquarters will consider transferring other divisions from the city.

We must reach a final decision within sixty days.

Since the maximum number of major points that most readers can remember is six or seven, keep your readers in mind as you frame your argument. Under the major points, group subordinate ideas in a manner calculated to help the reader understand and remember what you are saying. For brief messages, fewer points are supported by less detail. One summary—opening or closing—is enough.

Convince the reader immediately that what you are saying meets a need of his or hers. Then give all the information the reader requires. Being forthright (but not apologetic) about negative as well as positive aspects of the situation inspires trust and cuts down on requests for further clarification. Digressions and irrelevancies, however, adulterate the case being made and distract the reader.

Paragraphs and Sentences

Trust Your Eyes and Ears

Because pages composed primarily of short paragraphs look easy to read, they are more inviting than pages dense with long paragraphs. An occasional long paragraph, nonetheless, keeps the pace interesting—as do one- or two-sentence paragraphs when they stand out from the rest of the text.

Stick primarily to short sentences, too, but insert a few longer ones for the sake of pace. Short sentences are easier to write than long ones. While an expert writer can carry a reader gracefully through a sentence of many lines, intricately balancing phrases and clauses, a less skilled writer may get lost—and then so will the reader.

Keep topic sentences (those sentences that introduce a topic) succinct.

Writers in business are admonished by experts to use short words and avoid long ones. In general, this is sound advice. Yet, doesn't it make sense to use a long, familiar word instead of a short, obscure one? Isn't it better to use a long, difficult word that precisely conveys your meaning than a short, easy one that blurs the issue? An instantly recognized six-syllable word, like *responsibility*, for example, will not give a reader pause, whereas a technical three-syllable one, like *arbitrage*, may. There's nothing wrong with writing *arbitrage*, but brevity alone does not guarantee reader comprehension or interest.

GUIDELINES

- Use more six- to ten-line paragraphs than longer ones.
- Use more ten- to twenty-word sentences than longer ones.
- Use more one-, two-, and three-syllable words than longer ones.

A Passing Nod at Grammar

Paragraphs stray from monotony (which is in the desired direction) when they are composed of a combination of simple, complex, and compound sentences.

Depend most heavily on *simple sentences* because they are the easiest to write and to read.

> The profit-sharing plan is an unqualified success. It helps the firm hold on to outstanding managers.

Use *compound sentences* for related ideas that are of equal importance.

> The profit-sharing plan was a success right from the start, and it is as popular today as it ever was.

Use *complex sentences* for related ideas that are of *un*equal importance. The clause that can stand alone (italicized here) expresses the more important of the two ideas.

> *The profit-sharing plan*, which is ten years old, *helps the firm hold on to outstanding managers.*

Incomplete sentences add variety and create emphasis, but if used indiscriminately, they lose their punch.

> And become annoying. Which isn't what you want. At all. Under any circumstances.

Readers expect to find a subject and a predicate in a sentence. Incomplete sentences should be so short that this expectation is dashed immediately. Before it takes root.

Keep It Lean

There are several ways to reduce a paragraph that is too fat. Among them are these:

Shorten clauses to phrases or words.
The Association's philanthropy, which is extensive, will continue, *becomes:* The Association's extensive philanthropy will continue.

Shorten phrases to words.
At this point in time, *becomes:* Now.

Use the infinitive instead of a substitute.
He was hired for the purpose of developing a winning strategy, *becomes:* He was hired to develop a winning strategy.

Eliminate redundant words and ideas.
The consensus of opinion, *becomes:* The consensus.

Eliminate irrelevant words and ideas.
The new secretary is blond and types fast, *becomes:* The new secretary types fast.

In addition, you can pull from the major topic one or more ideas and put these ideas, with their supporting points, into a separate paragraph.

Break up long, convoluted sentences into two or more tight sentences or reduce them to one short sentence. Here are three examples.

1. Complicated, verbose sentences tend to weaken your argument, discourage full comprehension, and look intimidating on the page, as well as to reflect back badly on the writer, who is seen as not having stripped away distracting inessentials in order to bare the very heart of the matter, and who is also seen as not having presented lucidly what he most especially wants the reader or various readers to comprehend.

   This means: Wordiness exposes the writer's inadequacies as a writer.

2. Oil and gas companies that are quite small, and that formerly depended upon the high prices of oil and gas to enable them to stay solvent, had a harder and harder time getting credit—despite, in some cases, dedicated leadership—after the prices of both oil and gas started their downward slide.

   This means: Small oil and gas companies found it increasingly difficult to get credit, as oil and gas prices declined. Their managers are not necessarily to blame.

3. The Japanese, who are way out in front in the field of production of high-speed facsimile machines, have been successful in their attempts to solicit customers in this country.

   This means: As leaders in the production of high-speed facsimile machines, the Japanese have competed successfully in this country.

Transitions

Transitions, when properly handled, connect ideas, indicate relationships, and keep the reader's mind moving in tandem with the writer's. A transition (made by a word, phrase, clause, sentence, or paragraph) provides a bridge for the reader between the idea that precedes it and the idea that follows it.

HOW TRANSITIONAL WORDS FUNCTION

To amplify

Accordingly
Also
Because
Consequently
Eventually
For example
Formerly
Furthermore
In addition
In other words
In the same way
Moreover
Similarly
Simultaneously
Specifically
The next step
What's more
Without dissension

To continue

Again
Also
Another element
Because
Even so
Frequently
Granted
Generally
Indeed

In spite of
In some markets
Meanwhile
Of course
Simultaneously
Sooner or later
Therefore
Ultimately
Unfortunately

To contrast

But
Despite
Even so
However
Nonetheless
On the contrary
Otherwise
Rather than
Yet
Unless

To emphasize

Above all
Another key
As indicated
Beyond question
In other words

Most important	Inevitably
Once again	In the last analysis
Under no circumstances	In other words
Without a doubt	In short
	In spite of
To conclude	In sum
Accordingly	Nevertheless
A final consideration	The final effect
As a result	The implications
Cumulatively	Therefore
In conclusion	The results
In consequence	To recapitulate

Since the beginning of a sentence is a position of emphasis, place nonemphatic transitional words, phrases, or clauses in the middle.

Weak
> *Nevertheless*, we decline to close the deal.

Stronger
> We decline, *nevertheless*, to close the deal.

Emphatic
> *Under no circumstances* will we close the deal.

The repetition of concepts as well as of words can provide a transition. In the following paragraph, the idea of a management who appreciates creativity is related to the idea of creative marketing and distribution, through a reference to innovative (creative) product development.

> Our management understands the value of *creative* imagination. That's why our approach to marketing and distribution is every bit as *creative* as our approach to *innovative* product development.

Summing Up

When organizing business communications, use the five
W's. Adopt the time-honored dictum, "Tell readers what
you're going to say. Then say it. And then tell them what
you've said."

Do your homework.

Prefer short, simple words, sentences, and paragraphs to long ones—except where clarity is at stake.
Vary sentence structure, and provide readers with helpful
transitions.

Don't ask readers to remember more than six or seven
major points at a time. Imagine that you are the reader—
do you understand this communication clearly?

Make the Most of Emphasis and White Space

One of the most common errors is for the writer to use both sentences and paragraphs that are far too long. It is essential to get some light, some "breath" into the page.

Arthur N. Coleridge
Former Manager
Book Department
Readers Digest Association
London

A deft use of emphasis gives ideas appropriate weight and visually guides readers down the page, allowing them to see—

• What the main points are.
• How important each supporting point is.

Most of the techniques detailed here create emphasis while increasing the amount of white space on the page. Lots of white space makes a page look easy to read and to understand. A solid text, on the other hand, discourages readers.

Typography

CREATE EMPHASIS AND WHITE SPACE WITH:
   Numbered points
   Lettered points
   Bullets
   Dashes
   Underlining
   Capitalization
   Lines in the margins
   Paragraphs set in from left or both margins
   Boldface type
   Italics
   Color
   Boxes

A. Numbers, Letters, Bullets, and Dashes

Numbers, letters, bullets, and dashes help a reader to find subdivisions quickly. They are placed in any of three locations.

1. Isolated in the margin to the left of the text
   2. Flush left
      3. Indented

When you're using numbered points, tell the reader how many there will be. Numbers and letters are not used singly: two is the accepted minimum.
• One large bullet marks a more important point than . . . three small ones. A large bullet is made by typing an o and filling it in with ink.
   —A dash denotes a fairly insignificant point. Use the half-space typewriter key to fill in the space between two hyphens (—) or leave the space between the hyphens (--).

B. Underlining and Capitalization

Underlining and capitalization draw the reader's eye.
   Underline whole sentences; underlining each word separately indicates that italics are to be used in the final version.
   Capitalization has limited appeal. It is used mostly for headings of major sections of long texts. While it's offensive in a full sentence, it can be effective for individual words or phrases. For example—

The emerging nation's economy is gaining strength. In the last six months, the GROSS INTERNAL PRODUCT was up 6.7 percent, INDUSTRIAL ACTIVITY rose 11.2 percent, GOODS AND SERVICES soared 15 percent, and CONSTRUCTION climbed 10.3 percent.

C. Lines, Indentation, Typeface, Color, and Boxes

Lines drawn in the margin—in black and white or in color —accentuate notable features of a text for the reader.

Indented paragraphs, if they are short, group ideas where they can be found quickly and call attention to points you intend to stress.

Boldface, *italics*, and other variations in typeface are no longer restricted to printed material. Many typewriters now have interchangeable typing or printing elements. The printers used with word processors offer a choice of styles, too.

Add color with a colored typewriter ribbon, felt-tipped markers, or highlighters.

> Boxes make lists
> and summaries
> easy to locate.

Headings, Subheadings, and Titles

Good headings are short, succinct, informative, and consistent. They help to break up long texts by creating white space. They clarify and emphasize important points.

There are executives who admit to reading only headings and subheadings, so be sure yours lead the reader through salient points. Compose headings that present your argument logically and give your ideas due weight.

A heading is never used as the first sentence of the paragraph that follows it. (So the first sentence of this section begins not with, "They . . . ," referring to the heading as the antecedent, but with, "Good headings . . . .")

Headings are never used singly. If you need only one, use an underlined title, instead, to tell the reader right off what this is going to be about:

Dear Octavia Lowenthal:

November election: campaign fund raising activities

A title may also replace the antiquated and stuffy *Re.*

Headings and subheadings may gain from parallel construction. In the first example below, parallel construction is not used; in the second, it is. The second version is improved also by brevity and specificity.

1. NEW SUBSIDIARY, AFTER SLOW START, TURNS OUT TO BE SMART IDEA

   The Niche Research and Development Have Been Given Is One of Several Reasons

   Avoiding Government Intrusion

2. NEW SUBSIDIARY SUCCEEDS AS PROFIT CENTER

   Research and Development Are Stressed

   Products Stay Free of Government Regulation

Length and Position

Significant ideas receive greater prominence when they're discussed at greater length than less significant ones.

Short sentences and paragraphs stand out from longer ones.

Beginnings and endings furnish emphatic positions—which is why opening paragraphs often state the major theme while closing paragraphs recapitulate. The beginning and the end of each sentence and of each paragraph are emphatic. One speed-reading technique takes advantage of this: Only the first and last sentences of a paragraph are read at all.

Dominant and attractive ideas belong at the beginnings and ends of paragraphs. Stash bad news and minor or negative details in the middles of paragraphs.

Postscripts get noticed.

So does a word that is not found in its expected place:

What happens when a Japanese civil servant, age forty-five or older, is outranked by a younger colleague? *Retire he must.*

To soften the emphasis, write: *He must retire.*

Repetition and Punctuation

Words, phrases, and ideas that are repeated attract attention—as long as the repetition is purposeful rather than careless:

Yes: Feeding upon itself, *inflation* gives rise to corporate strategies that may further stimulate *inflation.*

Yes: She is a *sharp, sharp* stockbroker.

No: We must not let the *competitive* position of our largest *competitor* undermine our ability to *compete.*

Echoes created by repetition of groups of words not only contribute to the unity of the paragraph but also make the groups stand out:

The political risks are an unavoidable part of overseas investment. In planning overseas investment, all multinationals balance the probable returns against the unavoidable political risks.

Punctuation also may be a tool for creating emphasis. To make the sentence, *Get back to work now,* more emphatic, punctuate it in any of the following ways. Each example—except the last, which is snide—is slightly more emphatic than the preceding one.

Now, get back to work.
Now—get back to work.
Now: get back to work.
Get back to work. Now.
Now! Get back to work!
Get "back" to work now . . . .

advantages of
parenthetical
expression?
why not
rewrite
w/o
clauses

To enclose a parenthetical expression closely related to the main idea of the sentence, use commas.

To enclose a parenthetical expression that amplifies the main idea of the sentence, use (a) a single dash, (b) a pair of dashes, or (c) parentheses.

To emphasize a parenthetical expression, use a dash or a pair of dashes.

To emphasize the connection between two clauses, use a colon.

We were, to be honest, elated.

We were—when we heard of the victory—elated.

We were (thanks to the victory) elated.

Leclaire planned the victory—a victory that left them speechless.

Although victory took them to the Napa Valley, they found adventure there: They flew over the vineyards in a hot air balloon.

Quotation marks sometimes are mistakenly used for emphasis. Refrain from putting quotes around the word to be "stressed." Choose another emphatic form instead.

Use exclamation points sparingly.

Summing Up

Throughout your text, creating emphasis with a variety of techniques will guide the reader's eye and draw attention to your most notable ideas. Proper emphasis presents your organization of ideas in an obvious way, too.

Use plenty of white space to make a page appear non-threatening to readers.

8

How to Write Penetrating Sentences

In our business we receive dozens of memos and statistical reports every day from security analysts, portfolio managers, et al., and most of them are badly written. They use too much jargon, and their sentence structure is frequently convoluted.
William Gofen
Gofen and Glossberg

. . . three-fourths—if not nine-tenths—of bad writing in the world is bad because it fails to put its sentence elements logically together.
David Lambuth et al.
The Golden Book on Writing

To write skillfully and effectively, you need a friendly but not intimate acquaintance with grammar and usage. When you don't aspire to art, you need not master the subtleties of language that artists command. You need only manage a few essential elements deftly.

This chapter takes a pragmatic approach to construction in order to help you engage your reader's attention, understanding, interest, and cooperation.

PARTS OF A SENTENCE

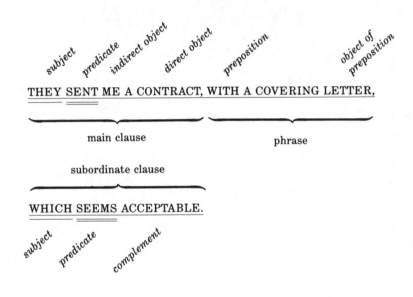

Parallel Construction

To alert your reader that ideas are similar—or that ideas contrast—express them in similar forms, using parallel construction.

No: The director of publicity is talented and reliable, but we're going to fire the head of the art department.

Yes: The director of publicity—who is talented and reliable—will stay, but the art director—who is mediocre and volatile—must go.

Apply prepositions, articles, and verbs consistently within a list.

No: We have offices *in* Boston, Houston, Dayton, and *in* San Diego.

Yes: We have offices *in* Boston, Houston, Dayton, and San Diego.

No: There is nothing on his desk except *a* telephone, carafe, *one* ashtray, and *the* photo of his racehorse.

Yes: There is nothing on his desk except *a* telephone, *a* carafe, *an* ashtray, and *a* photo of his racehorse.

No: The regional sales manager's job—
  1. *Assist* the director of sales.
  2. *Be* the field staff supervisor.
  3. Cost budgets *must be prepared*.
  4. Sales forecasts *are* part of this job.

Yes: The regional sales manager—
1. *Assists* the director of sales.
2. *Supervises* the field staff.
3. *Prepares* cost budgets.
4. *Designs* sales forecasts.

Whenever possible, with expressions such as *first . . . second,* or *either . . . or,* use the same construction for what follows.

No: *First,* I want to thank you for your order, and *second,* you have chosen well.

Yes: I want *first* to thank you for your order and *second* to commend you on your choice.

No: She's *both* a forceful leader *and* flexible.

Yes: As a leader, she's *both* forceful *and* flexible.

A sentence may read more smoothly if its clauses have the same subject.

Acceptable
Because *she* was a loner and not a team player, *management* was disenchanted with her.

Improved
Because *she* was a loner and not a team player, *she* did not score with management.

Active Verbs

Active verbs are stronger than passive verbs. An active verb tells what a subject is doing.

> They made an offer.

A passive verb tells what is being done to the subject.

> An offer was made by them.

Passive verbs are easy to spot because they include some form of the verb *to be*.

Strong writing requires active verbs. Limit your use of passive verbs to the infrequent occasions when they will serve you well.

A *passive verb* may be used to advantage when—

You don't want to name the doer of the action.

Passive   The alternatives have been exhausted.

Active   You blew it.

You don't know the doer of the action.

Passive   The fire alarm was set off by mistake.

Active   Someone set off the fire alarm by mistake.

You want to give the receiver of the action more importance than the doer of the action.

Passive   Our brand name is widely recognized.

Active   Many people recognize our brand name.

An *active verb* has these advantages over a passive verb—

It conveys conviction.

Passive   The project is expected to be completed on time.

<u>*Active*</u>   We expect to complete the project on time.

It is personal rather than impersonal.

Passive   It's believed that you are deserving of a promotion.

<u>*Active*</u>   I believe you deserve a promotion.

It acknowledges responsibility.

Passive   You were misjudged.

<u>*Active*</u>   I misjudged you.

It can shorten a sentence made longer than necessary by passive verbs.

Passive   Merchandise was marked down because of poor retail sales.

<u>*Active*</u>   Poor retail sales forced markdowns of merchandise.

Substituting an active verb for (a) a noun or (b) an adjective or (c) some form of *to be* strengthens your prose.

(a)

Weak

Let's take a *meeting* by the pool for a *discussion* of the property.

Strong

Let's *meet* by the pool and *discuss* the property.

(b)

Weak

Our indoctrination program is *helpful* to new employees.

Strong

Our indoctrination program *helps* new employees.

(c)

Weak

Depreciation *should be* on the straight-line method.

Strong

Straight-line depreciation *works* best.

Order

If you're having trouble assembling a sentence, try rearranging its parts according to (a) chronology, (b) cause and effect, (c) importance, (d) procedure—or any other logical order.

Illogical	*Logical*
(a) She walked briskly to the building after parking her car in her assigned space.	After parking her car in her assigned space, she walked briskly to the building.
(b) They shook hands, pleased with the agreement.	Pleased with the agreement, they shook hands.

Illogical	*Logical*
(c) Because of his outstanding qualifications, he got the job.	He got the job because of his outstanding qualifications.
(d) You'll solve the problem once you've analyzed it and developed a plan of action.	Analyze the problem and develop a plan to solve it.

When you place the main clause of a sentence at the end, near the period, you write a *periodic sentence*. In the examples below, the main clause is italicized.

Short periodic sentences are useful in creating variety, orderliness, or, as here, emphasis—

Determined to prevail, *she marched into the meeting*.

Long periodic sentences tax a reader's patience, unless the climax is strong enough to warrant the suspense.

Through emphasis on diversification, acquisition, and original technology, *the corporate venture group takes high risks*.

Despite pounding heart, trembling hands, and dry mouth, *she spoke with aplomb*.

Modifiers

Modifiers are words, phrases, or clauses that amplify the meanings of other words, phrases, or clauses. They belong close to whatever they modify, where they will clarify.

The following examples illustrate how moving a modifier changes the meaning of a sentence. Modifiers are italicized here.

Modifying word

We believe this incentive *alone* will motivate major industries to conserve energy.

We *alone* believe this incentive will motivate major industries to conserve energy.

Modifying phrase

Filled with hope and confidence, he sent his resumé to a dozen companies.

He sent his resumé, *filled with hope and confidence*, to a dozen companies.

He sent his resumé to a dozen companies *filled with hope and confidence*.

Modifying clause

The planners, *who prefer extreme solutions*, were encouraged by top management.

The planners were encouraged by top management, *who prefer extreme solutions*.

Misplaced Modifiers

A misplaced modifier is one that is placed so far away from the word or words it relates to that the sentence is confusing. In this sentence, it's unclear whether the takeover occurred at lunch or was to be analyzed at lunch—

> They agreed to analyze the takeover *at lunch*.

Here, the modifier is handled correctly—

> They agreed that *at lunch* they would analyze the take-over.

One of the best and easiest ways to achieve sentence variety is to shift the relationship of the modifiers to the subject and predicate. A short periodic sentence, in which the modifiers come near the beginning, offers a reader relief from the standard pattern of subject-predicate-modifiers. It's generally desirable, however, to keep subject and predicate reasonably close together.

> *Having been widely circulated*, the <u>report</u> <u>triggered</u> an investigation.
> The <u>report</u>, *having been widely circulated*, <u>triggered</u> an investigation.

Both versions of the preceding sentence make sense. Either might be chosen, for the sake of variety.

Dangling Modifiers

A dangling modifier is a modifier that does not modify anything. To rescue dangling modifiers, give them the correct words to modify. Modified words are underlined and modi-⌉ fiers are italicized in the examples that follow.

wrong what does the action

Dangling Construction
Wresting control of the company through a proxy fight, management was bypassed.

Corrected

> *Wresting control of the company through a proxy fight,* he bypassed management.

Dangling Construction

> *Comparing the computer revolution to the industrial revolution,* union members were urged to study mi-croelectronics.

Corrected

> *Comparing the computer revolution to the industrial* revolution, she urged union members to study micro-electronics.

Dangling Construction

> *After joining the cable television market,* intense com-petition faced the station.

Corrected

> *After joining the cable television market,* the station faced intense competition.

Dangling Construction

> *During his self-improvement phase,* the executive gym was relaxing.

Corrected

> *During his self-improvement phase,* he relaxed at the executive gym.

Dangling Construction

> *Slick and ambitious,* office politics came naturally to her.

Corrected

> *Slick and ambitious,* she was a natural at office politics.

Dangling Construction

> *To post a profit,* costs had been cut.

Corrected
> *To post a profit,* <u>they</u> had cut costs.

The use of *which, this,* or *that* to modify an entire clause or sentence is vague. Be specific.

Vague
> The underground economy has grown twice as fast as the gross national product, *which* suggests that it has not been hit by the recession.

Vague
> The underground economy has grown twice as fast as the gross national product. *This* (or *that*) suggests that it has not been hit by the recession.

Corrected
> The underground economy apparently has not been hit by the recession, for it has grown twice as fast as the gross national product.

Restrictive and Nonrestrictive Clauses

~~that~~   • which
          • always   commas

          • remove commas → changed
                                      meaning

Certain television programs are preceded by a warning that the material they contain may not be suitable for all viewers. Consider yourself warned that the material on restrictive and nonrestrictive clauses may be too technical for some readers.

The difference between a nonrestrictive clause or phrase and a restrictive clause or phrase is important to effective writers because—

- Nonrestrictive clauses and phrases are always set off by commas, but restrictive clauses and phrases are set off by commas only if they precede the main clause.
- If the commas enclosing nonrestrictive clauses and phrases are dropped—but nothing else is changed—the meanings of the sentences are changed.
- Whether to use *which* or *that* at the beginning of a clause is determined by whether the clause is nonrestrictive or restrictive.

Consider this nonrestrictive sentence—

The accountant, who arrived early, is new to the firm.

Because the clause is nonrestrictive and so is enclosed in commas, the sentence may be rewritten as two sentences without changing the meaning:

The accountant is new to the firm. She arrived early.

However, to distinguish the new accountant from other accountants—who arrived later and have been employed longer—merely drop the commas, creating a restrictive sentence (which cannot be rewritten without changing the meaning):

The accountant who arrived early is new to the firm.

All you usually need to do to decide whether or not a clause or phrase is nonrestrictive is to try to break the sentence into two sentences. If you succeed, without changing the meaning, then you've got a nonrestrictive clause or phrase.

Restrictive Phrase Following Main Clause
They will decide *after their conference*.

Restrictive Phrase Preceding Main Clause
After their conference, they will decide.

Nonrestrictive Phrase
Pat, *oblivious to the weather*, opened the window.

Which and *that* are not interchangeable: *which* introduces a nonrestrictive clause, and *that* introduces a restrictive clause.

> The contracts, *which* were just renegotiated, will run for three years.

This nonrestrictive sentence simply means that—

> The contracts will run for three years. They were just renegotiated.

If the commas are dropped from this sentence and *which* is replaced by *that*, then the meaning changes, and the sentence becomes restrictive:

> The contracts *that* were just renegotiated will run for three years.

This version means that the contracts that will run for three years are the ones that were just renegotiated, as opposed to other contracts.

Summing Up

Construct strong sentences by manipulating their elements. Use active rather than passive verbs most of the time. Give modifiers something to modify and place them close to the modified words. Handle restrictive and nonrestrictive sentences knowingly.

Give readers the information they need in a form that will help them give you what you need.

9

Manipulating the Parts of Speech

[He] said he does not look at the houses before he advertises them in the newspaper. Asked how he knows they are "adorable" or "splendid," he answered: "It's adjectives. Every person in every business up and down El Cajon uses adjectives. It's part of advertising. If it wasn't for adjectives we wouldn't be in business. Adjectives are what make us smarter than the average person."

A reprint in the New Yorker
from the San Diego Union

THE EIGHT PARTS OF SPEECH

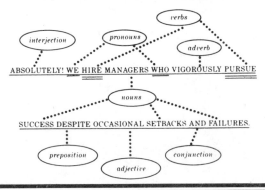

T his chapter can help you to avoid pitfalls associated
with each of the eight parts of speech. For more detailed rules of grammar, consult a good grammar guide.*
And remember that readers may condemn those who make
errors in grammar but will never think less of those who
write correctly.

Verbs

The wider an infinitive is split, the more readers are of-
fended.

Maybe: *To* brazenly *split* an infinitive with even a single
word is *to* immediately *lose* ground with the most
particular of readers.

No: *To* thoughtlessly and without remorse *split* an infinitive with a string of words is *to* cavalierly and
insensitively, one might even say self-destructively,
lose ground with the most tolerant of readers.

Yes: Not *to split* an infinitive is *to offend* no one.

Don't ask readers to hold the first part of a multiword
verb in mind through several other words before you reveal the complete verb.

Taxing
They *might*, in the long run, *have* enthusiastically and
confidently *elected* him to the board.

* See "Helpful Books," pp. 112–113.

Corrected

In the long run, they *might have elected* him to the board enthusiastically and confidently.

It's common knowledge that a single subject takes a single predicate. Often, when writers fail to achieve this agreement, they haven't stopped to think about what the actual subject of the sentence is. Take the time to be sure that you have not been careless.

No: The complete <u>line</u> of desk accessories <u>are</u> on display.
Yes: The complete <u>line</u> of desk accessories <u>is</u> on display.

No: Either the <u>comedian</u> or his <u>writers</u> <u>is</u> responsible.
Yes: Either the <u>comedian</u> or his <u>writers</u> <u>are</u> responsible.

No: There <u>is</u> enormous <u>advantages</u> in doing it her way.
Yes: There <u>are</u> enormous <u>advantages</u> in doing it her way.

Use *got,* not *gotten.* As the late Jacob Henrici—a distinguished Pittsburgh bookseller—was wont to say, "*Gotten* has got to go."

Nouns

Certain nouns look plural but may be singular, depending on usage.

<u>Politics</u> <u>is</u> his passion.
Corporate <u>politics</u> <u>are</u> fascinating.

Statistics is a difficult subject.
Statistics are unreliable.

Columbia Records has prestige.

Other nouns look singular but may be plural, depending on usage.

The number of openings remains fluid.
A number of questions come to mind.

Management agrees in principle.
Management disagree among themselves.

Stringing together a bunch of nouns blurs their meaning. Nouns are italicized here.

No: Here is a *list* of *suggestions* for *solutions* to *problems* of *housing* in the *city* and *suburbs.*

Yes: Here is a *list* of *suggestions* for solving urban and suburban housing *problems.*

Pronouns

The subject pronouns are: *I, we, you, she, he, it, they*
The object pronouns are: *me, us, you, her, him, it, them*
Pronouns give many people trouble. Here, some of the more common kinds of errors have been corrected.

No: It is *me*.

Yes: It is *I*.

   (*I am the person*, *not*, *Me is the person*.)

No: Each participant did *their* part.*

Yes: Each participant did *her* or *his* part.

   (*Participant* is singular.)

No: No one forgot to submit *their* expense accounts.*

Yes: No one forgot to submit *his* or *her* expense account.

   (*No one* is singular.)

No: You're as well qualified as *me*.

Yes: You're as well qualified as *I*.

   (*You're as well qualified as I am well qualified.*)

No: *Me* and Oliver volunteered.

No: *I* and Oliver volunteered.

Yes: Oliver and *I* volunteered.

   (*I volunteered*, not, *Me volunteered*; and don't put yourself first.)

No: She invested in a bull *who* could improve her stock.

Yes: She invested in a bull *that* could improve her stock.

   (*Who* refers only to people.)

No: Assign *whomever* will do the best job.

Yes: Assign *whoever* will do the best job.

   (*Whoever* is the subject of <u>*will do*</u>.)

* Although the *Oxford English Dictionary* condones this usage where the sex of
the person referred to is unknown, most fussy readers do not condone it.

No: He is the mentor to *who* I owe everything.

Yes: He is the mentor to *whom* I owe everything.

(*Whom* is the object of *to*.)

No: *Us* managers must write forcefully.

Yes: *We* managers must write forcefully.

(*We . . . must write . . . .*)

No: Crandon is supposed to share a secretary with Troy, but *he* monopolizes *him*.

Yes: Crandon monopolizes the secretary whom *he* is supposed to share with Troy.

(*He* and *him* are ambiguous in the first version.)

No: Josh gave the assignment to Eric, Janet, and *I*.

Yes: Josh gave the assignment to Eric, Janet, and *me*.

(*Me* is the object of *to*. You wouldn't say, "Josh gave the assignment to *I*.")

No: Ethel asked Marty, Gene, and *I* to submit suggestions.

Yes: Ethel asked Marty, Gene, and *me* to submit suggestions.

(*Me* is the object of *asked*. Not, "Ethel asked *I*.")

Note:

He consults you more often than <u>she</u>, *means:* He consults you more often than <u>she</u> consults you; *but* He consults you more often than <u>her</u>, *means:* He consults you more often than he consults <u>her</u>.

Each other refers to two. *One another* refers to three or more.

Refrain from giving a country a gender.
The United States and *its* (not *her*) allies.

Adjectives and Adverbs

Adjectives and adverbs are sometimes mistaken for each other, especially when they appear after verbs referring to the five senses.

I feel badly, *means:* My sense of touch is inadequate.
   [*Badly* is an adverb.]

I feel bad, *means:* I feel sorry, *or:* I feel sick.
   [*Bad* is an adjective.]

   She looks well, *means:* She searches carefully, *or:* She appears to be healthy.
   [*Well* may be an adverb or an adjective.]
   Some adjectives are tricky:

Less refers to amount, *fewer* to number.

   This office could use *less* air conditioning.
   This office could use *fewer* air conditioners.

Continuous action continues without interruption.
Continual action continues with brief interruptions.

Use *former* and *latter* only to compare two.

   I could have played golf or tennis. I chose the *latter*.
   I could have played golf, tennis, or volleyball. I chose the *last*.

   Absolute adjectives, like *unique, essential, foremost, complete*, and *maximum* cannot be modified, qualified, or compared—simply because they *are* absolute.

No: He's a *very unique* lawyer.
Yes: He's a *unique* lawyer.

No: That's the *most essential* element.
Yes: That's the *essential* element.

It makes obvious sense, however, to write—

> That's the *most nearly* (or *least nearly*) *essential* element.

Sort and *kind* are singular and take *this* or *that; sorts* and *kinds* are plural and take *these* and *those.*

No: I prefer *those kind* of *editors.*
Yes: I prefer *those kinds* of *editors* [or *that kind of editor*].

The comparative degree serves for two items and the superlative degree for three or more items.

> Claudia and Nora are both bright, but Nora is the *brighter.*
>
> Claudia, Nora, and Edna are all bright, but Nora is the *brightest.*

Listen to what you have written. Does it make sense? For instance—

> No one on the team is as good as he is,

means, literally, that not even he is as good as he is, if he's on the team. The sentence should read—

> No one *else* on the team is as good as he is.

It is colloquially correct to use the adverb modifier, *more,* without stating what it modifies, but careful writers avoid the practice.

Colloquial

The mayor demands *more* from you than from me.

Careful

The mayor demands *more substance and energy* from you than from me.

It is true that *and, but, for, nor, or, yet,* and *so* are ordinarily conjunctions.

But they also may be used as transitional adverbs at the beginning of a sentence or paragraph.

Conjunctions

Common errors in the use of conjunctions have been corrected in these examples:

If does not mean *whether*.

No: He does not know *if* he will be reelected.

Yes: He does not know *whether* he will be reelected.
(Part of this sentence is omitted but implied: *He does not know whether* or not *he will be reelected*.)

Like is not a conjunction. Never use *like* where *as if* may be substituted.

No: She talks *like* she knows her subject.

Yes: She talks *as if* (or *as though*) she knows her subject.

Yes: She talks *like* one who knows her subject.

Yes: She talks *like* an expert.

Write: The reason is <u>that</u>....

Not: The reason is <u>because</u>.... (or, The reason is <u>why</u>....)

In a comparison requiring both *than* and *as*, don't try to make one of them do the work of both.

No: The first announcer's voice is *as* deep, if not deeper *than*, the second announcer's voice.

Yes: The first announcer's voice is *as* deep *as*, if not deeper *than*, the second announcer's voice.

Interjections

Although exclamation points frequently make the writer sound hysterical, they are commonly associated with interjections.

Blasted! Horse feathers! Wow! Right on! Perfect!

Prepositions

Where words in relation take two different prepositions, don't omit either preposition.

No: He is better and more interested *in* keeping the records than I am.

Yes: He is better *at* and more interested *in* keeping records than I am.

To spare your readers possible confusion, repeat a preposition before each phrase or clause to which it relates.

Give the test *to* the first group now and *to* the second group later.

Is it all right to end a sentence with a preposition? Sure it is—if moving the preposition away from the end makes your sentence stiff or awkward. But the end of a sentence is a place of emphasis, and a preposition is seldom an attention grabber.

Careless
The convention was all she talked *about.*
Careful
All she talked *about* was the convention.

Stiff
That's an accomplishment *of* which to be proud.
Natural
That's an accomplishment to be proud *of.*

You are judged by critical readers in part by your handling of idiomatic prepositions. Here are some—

IDIOMS TO REMEMBER

Incorrect	*Correct*
Alongside of	Alongside
Center around	Center in, center on, revolve around
Convicted for	Convicted of
Die from	Die of
Excerpt of	Excerpt from
Forbidden from	Forbidden to
Arrive *around* seven P.M.	Arrive *about* seven P.M.

Other idioms involving prepositions include—

* *Accuse of, charge with.*

* *Among* for three or more people, things, or ideas.
  Between for two people, things, or ideas.

* *Beside* means *close to.*
  Besides means *in addition to.*

* *Compared to* for likening people things, or ideas.
  Compared with for discussing similarities and differences.

  The visitor *compared* our reception room *to* an art gallery.
  The board *compared* James *with* other candidates.

* *Due to* never means *because of.*

  No: *Due to* the strike, production slowed down.
  Yes: *Because of* the strike, production slowed down.

* *Kind of* does not take an article.

No: Some *kind of an* electronic device.
Yes: Some *kind of* electronic device.

- *Of* never correctly replaces *have*.

  No: I *could of been* a contender.
  Yes: I *could have been* a contender.

- *Onto* is a preposition describing a position upon. *On to* is an adverbial phrase.

  He rolled his wheelchair *onto* the elevator.
  He rolled *on to* a better job.

- *Round* never *means around*.

  No: Here we go round the mulberry bush.

     When in doubt about a preposition, look it up in a list of idioms.*

Summing Up

Employ the parts of speech correctly, and avoid common mistakes in grammar that, in a reader's mind, label you as careless.

* See "Helpful Books," pp. 112–113.

Don't split infinitives; do see that subjects and predicates agree; pay attention to pronouns; don't confuse adjectives with adverbs; use conjunctions accurately and interjections conservatively; be precise in the idiomatic use of prepositions.

When in doubt about a point of grammar, look it up.

How to Start and How to Finish

The worst thing about writing is getting started.
                                    William M. Fine
                                    President
                                    Dan River Mills

Most writing is too long because it's easier to ramble on than to compose and edit a concise written message.

        Wallace W. Elton
        Senior Vice President
        International Executive Service Corps

T o produce a winning piece of writing, you have first to overcome any resistance you feel to the act of writing and finally to reread and revise whatever you write. These two facets of effective writing are explored here, so you won't waste either your own or your reader's time.

How to Surmount Writer's Block

Writer's block is a hurdle, not a barrier, between you and the reader. Once you've jumped it and started writing, you'll gain momentum that should carry you along to the finish.

Writer's block may appear in several shapes to impede you. It may—

Distract you with nonessential interruptions.
Immobilize you as you stare at the blank page, your mind also a blank.
Seduce you into delays and daydreams.

Writer's block is a psychological block. What to do? Here are fourteen suggestions.

Time management

1. Set aside time to write. Tell your secretary to hold all calls. Explain to colleagues that you can't be interrupted during this period. Allowing yourself to be interrupted when you're writing has several disadvantages: Interruptions encourage you to lose your train of thought and to make errors; they force you to start writing again—repeatedly—after each new interruption; by interfering with

your concentration, they reduce the probability that you will get the desired results. When you cannot avoid interruptions, keep them few in number and brief in duration.

2. Write at one sitting everything you need to write on that day. The motion of the first effort should propel you through subsequent ones.

3. Where is it inscribed that you must be at your desk to contemplate drafting a letter, memo, or report? Thinking about the task at odd moments (on an airplane, in a sauna) helps you face a blank page with ideas at the ready.

4. Reduce the amount of writing you do. Ask yourself what a reply to a letter or memo you've received will accomplish. If you answer yourself, *nothing*, or, *not much*, don't write. The time you save by not answering low-priority paper may be devoted to high-priority writing.

5. After reading correspondence, make notes directly on the letters and memos that you've decided merit answers. Or dictate replies—or notes for replies—then and there. This method is recommended by time management experts because it reduces the number of times you handle and think about paper.

6. Be flexible about hours. If you think most clearly by dawn's early light, engage in significant writing then. If you're a night owl, become a night writer.

Preparation

7. Thoroughly planning an important piece of writing simplifies writing it. Work closely from detailed notes, an outline, and perhaps a diagram. With casual projects, jot down the main points to be included, then write from those notes.

8. Frame a question that is answered by this letter, memo, or report. Reply by writing without pause—for a page or two, or for three to five minutes. Don't cross out, edit, or hesitate. Afterward, underline any good ideas you brought forth and pull them together in more finished prose.

9. When you're hopelessly entangled in your own thoughts and words, imagine a colleague asking you to explain what you're writing about. Next, imagine yourself answering; if you're comfortable talking to yourself, answer aloud. Write down that answer, then expand and refine it.

10. When there is a lot to say, getting started may be difficult. Writer's block is more apt to obstruct complex, formal, or lengthy pieces of writing than casual ones. Try writing a couple of easy memos before tackling a difficult assignment.

11. Read an interesting article in a journal in your field, as a warm-up exercise. Read the *Wall Street Journal* for its exemplary style. Read in any nonfiction book that stimulates you. Then begin to write.

12. For a major task, set a deadline; set smaller goals as well. Give yourself a quota of pages to finish each day. Mark the dates on your calendar by which each section should be completed. Working toward smaller goals may help you to meet the deadline with composure.

Frame of mind

13. Physical exertion clears the head. Can you find time for a brisk walk around the block? How about climbing a couple of flights of stairs? Even a round trip to the water cooler may provide a preamble* to sitting down and thinking on paper.

14. Do you meditate or practice relaxing exercises? Then draw on these resources to free your mind of distractions before beginning to write.

---

* Puns are risky.

Editorial Checklist for Managers

The best writers rewrite and cut. Editing and revising are, fortunately, easier than writing.

Conscientious managers reread everything they write, from simple memos to complicated reports—for tone, meaning, accuracy, and language. Some managers also ask colleagues to look over an important piece of writing and suggest changes.

Edit with conventional proofreader's marks as they are shown in any reliable manual of style.*

The length and significance of what you are writing will determine how many points you consider from the checklist given here.

Procedure

☐ Put away for a day or two the first draft of a long text.

☐ Then read what you've written, assessing it for meaning and logic.

☐ While you're working on meaning and logic, mark rough spots in language, but don't fix them until later.

☐ After you're satisfied that your meaning and logic are clear, read through again for language.

☐ Don't let your writer's ego inhibit your editor's eye and ear: Separate yourself as writer from yourself as editor.

☐ Unless you're revising on a word processor or on an electronic typewriter that has text-editing functions, use scissors and tape or staples to transpose ideas.

---

* See "Helpful Books," pp. 112–113.

☐ When you're experimenting with the sequence of ideas, leave room to rewrite transitions that will indicate new relationships.

Meaning and logic

☐ Is your progress from opening to closing paragraph so obvious that the reader will always understand how each point relates to the main theme?

☐ Does your introduction tell the reader what you are going to say and how you are going to say it?

☐ Does your conclusion tell the reader what you have said?

☐ Are major and minor points easily identifiable?

☐ Do major and minor points relate logically to each other from the beginning through the middle to the end?

☐ Are transitions helpful? Do they promote a lively pace?

☐ Are any paragraphs overburdened with too many ideas?

☐ Is your argument clarified or muddled by the changes, when you experiment with the sequence of ideas?

☐ Have you maintained a uniform point of view and a coherent argument?

☐ Are the conclusions justified by the argument?

☐ Does each paragraph or section that starts with a topic sentence fulfill its promise?

☐ If you cover several topics, can you deal with any of them more effectively either in additional sections or in a separate communication?

☐ Have you presented your subject without distortion and in a plausible way?

☐ Have you avoided abstractions and unsupported generalizations?

☐ Is factual information complete, correct, and specific?

124 *Writing That Means Business*

- [ ] Can you analyze and fix the problem if your mind wanders at the same spot repeatedly?
- [ ] Have you stressed the positive aspect of your subject, eliminating negative words and ideas?
- [ ] Have you stated deadlines and the dates by which actions are to be performed?
- [ ] Have you doublechecked: facts, figures, dates, quotations, and documentation? Thoroughly?
- [ ] Have you cut out: exaggeration, euphemisms, hedging, disclaimers, evasion, anger, jargon, irrelevancies, and redundancies?
- [ ] When in doubt about cutting—cut, reread—and replace what you've cut only if it adds something.

Emphasis

- [ ] Does your use of typographical emphasis give proper weight to your ideas? Is it consistent?
- [ ] Is there plenty of white space?
- [ ] Are headings and subheadings typographically consistent?
- [ ] In long communications, summarize your argument with the logical arrangement of headings and subheadings.

The reader

- [ ] Have you appealed to the reader's enlightened self-interest?
- [ ] Does your tone strike the right balance between familiarity and formality?
- [ ] Are any attempts at humor successful?
- [ ] Have you been tactful and diplomatic?

☐ Are you satisfied that your words will not be misinterpreted?

☐ Is everything the reader needs to know about the subject included?

☐ Address your reader's level of expertise, and define technical words, abbreviations, and acronyms.

Language

☐ Are modifiers placed close to what they modify? Do they all have something to modify?

☐ Has parallel construction been used where it is demanded?

☐ Are your sentences structurally varied, with words, phrases, and clauses in the best possible order?

☐ Are nonrestrictive clauses and restrictive clauses handled correctly?

☐ Have you avoided split infinitives and the separation of multiword verbs?

☐ Is there agreement between subjects and predicates and between pronouns and the nouns they're related to?

☐ Do your words express your exact meaning?

☐ Did you read aloud what you wrote and fix any part that sounded choppy, ambiguous, awkward, or confused?

☐ Have you used active verbs except when a passive verb gives a definite advantage?

☐ Have you used strong verbs?

☐ Have you avoided sexism and clichés?

☐ Have you clarified ambiguous wording and checked your handling of idioms?

☐ Have you cut out all words that can be spared? Tightened verbose sentences?

☐ Did you look up correct grammar, punctuation, spelling, and usage when you were uncertain about them?

☐ After you've fixed something, read the new version in case a major error prevented your noticing other errors.

Summing Up

Writer's block needn't stymie you if you will set aside time to write, then prepare to write, and finally, get into a frame of mind conducive to writing.

At the other end, edit and revise for tone, meaning, brevity, accuracy, directness, logic, emphasis, and language.

Above all, ask yourself if the message you intend to send will be accessible easily to the reader.

Afterword

There are technologically advanced offices where some correspondence never gets onto paper. Letters and memos
are sent from computer to computer—and the reader, not
the writer, decides whether or not to put the message into
hard copy or erase it from the screen after it has been read.
Readers, then, become ever more critical—and writers
must be prepared to meet the challenge.

*The ability to write well is like ability in any field. If you
write or do things better than others, you will certainly
have a competitive edge.*

> J. K. Jamieson
> *Former CEO and Chairman*
> *Exxon Corporation*

Helpful Books

A selection of reliable reference books on language is more necessity than luxury for managers who write.

Allen, F. Sturges. *Allen's Synonyms and Antonyms.* Edited by T.H. Vail Motter. New York: Harper & Row, 1949.
Why use the same word over and over—or why use a stuffy word—when you can look up a substitute?

Bernstein, Theodore M. *Reverse Dictionary.* Collaborator, Jane Wagner. New York: Times Books, 1975.
An alphabetical list of definitions, with words given to fit each one.

Ehrlich, Eugene; Flexner, Stuart Berg; Carruth, Gorton; and Hawkins, Joyce M., eds. *Oxford American Dictionary.* New York: Oxford University Press, 1980 (hardcover); Avon Books, 1980 (paperback).
The usage notes and "Index to Entries with Usage Notes" make this volume invaluable; it is also a first-rate dictionary.

Holcombe, Marya W., and Stein, Judith K. *Writing for Decision Makers: Memos and Reports with a Competitive Edge.* Belmont: Lifetime Learning Publications, 1981.
Detailed directions for planning, writing, and revising reports and for locating, analyzing, and solving problems. Would be even more useful with an index.

Jordan, Lewis, ed. *The New York Times Manual of Style and Usage.* New York: Times Books, 1976.

A Manual of Style. 13th ed. Chicago: The University of Chicago Press, 1982.

McWilliams, Peter A. *The Word Processing Book: A Short Course in Computer Literacy.* Los Angeles: Prelude Press, 1982.

Miller, Casey, and Swift, Kate. *The Handbook of Nonsexist Writing.* New York: Lippincott & Crowell, 1980.

Quinn, Jim. *American Tongue and Cheek: A Populist Guide to Our Language.* New York: Pantheon Books, 1980 (hardcover); Penguin Books, 1982 (paperback).
Lively reading that may relax writers who don't care to be language snobs. Mr. Quinn takes soundly researched exception to rules of grammar and usage insisted on by purists, and he has a high old time doing it.

Roget's International Thesaurus. 4th ed., rev. Robert L. Chapman. New York: Thomas Y. Crowell Co., 1977.

Roman, Kenneth, and Raphaelson, Joel. *Writing That Works: How to write memos, letters, reports, speeches, resumes, plans and other papers that say what you mean—and get things done.* New York: Harper & Row, 1981.
The authors—senior officers of Ogilvy & Mather—have a breezy style that makes their sound advice easy to understand and to remember. Would be even more useful with an index.

Strunk, William, Jr., and White, E.B. *The Elements of Style.* New York: Macmillan Publishing Co., 1959.

The Written Word II. Based on *The American Heritage Dictionary.* Boston: Houghton Mifflin Co., 1983.
This little guide to grammar, punctuation, spelling, form, and usage is organized so neatly that it is easy to use. It includes a section on forms of address.

Zinsser, William. *On Writing Well.* New York: Harper & Row, 1980 (hardcover); Harper Colophon Books, 1980 (paperback).

See, also, any book by either Edwin Newman or William Safire. These entertaining gurus of contemporary American English sharpen our awareness of the use—and misuse—of language.

Bibliography

Annual Reports, 1981, of these companies: Arizona Public Service Company; Avnet, Inc.; Palm Beach Incorporated; Puget Power; Warner Communications.

Beam, Henry H. "Good Writing: An Underrated Executive Skill." *Human Resources Management.* Spring 1981.

Beaudouin, John T., and Mattlin, Everett. *The Phrase-Dropper's Handbook.* New York: Doubleday & Co., 1976 (hardcover); Dell Publishing Co., 1977 (paperback).

Bolles, Richard Nelson. *What Color Is Your Parachute? A Practical Manual for Job-Hunters & Career Changers.* 1982 ed. Berkeley: Ten Speed Press, 1982.

Bovee, Courtland L. *Business Writing Workshop: A Study Guide of Readings and Exercises for More Effective Letters, Memos, and Reports.* Originally published by Kendall/Hunt Publishing Company, 1976. Reprint. San Diego, Calif.: Roxbury Publishing Co., 1980.

Brady, Sue A. "Better Business Writing." Seminar manual prepared for Dun & Bradstreet, Inc., New York, 1981. Photocopied.

Braun, Carl F. *Letter-Writing in Action.* Alhambra: C. F. Braun & Co., 1951.

130

Bibliography 131

Buzan, Tony. *Use Both Sides of Your Brain*. New York: Dutton, 1983.

Dunkle, Terry. "Crosscurrents: Obfuscatory Scrivenery (Foggy Writing)." *Science '82*. April: 82–84.

Ehrlich, Eugene; Flexner, Stuart Berg; Carruth, Gorton; and Hawkins, Joyce M., eds. *Oxford American Dictionary*. New York: Oxford University Press, 1980 (hardcover); Avon Books, 1980 (paperback).

Flesch, Rudolf. *How to Write, Speak, and Think More Effectively*. New York: New American Library, A Signet Book (paperback), 1964.

————. *How to Write Plain English: A Book for Lawyers and Consumers*. New York: Harper & Row, 1979.

General Services Administration. *Plain Letters: Records Management Handbook*. Washington, D.C.: Superintendent of Documents, U.S. Government Printing Office.

Hearst, William Randolph. *The Newspaper Credo*. Hearst Consolidated Publications, 1959.

Hemphill, Phyllis Davis. *Business Communications with Writing Improvement Exercises*. 2nd ed. Anita M. Hemphill, ed. Englewood Cliffs, N.J. Prentice-Hall, 1981.

Hillman, Howard. *The Art of Writing Business Reports and Proposals*. Coauthor, Lisa Loring. New York: Vanguard Press, 1981.

Holcombe, Marya, W. and Stein, Judith K. *Writing for Decision Makers: Memos and Reports with a Competitive Edge*. Belmont, Calif.: Lifetime Learning Publications, 1981.

Johnson, Eric W. *How to Achieve Competence in English: A Quick-Reference Handbook*. New York: Bantam Books, 1976.

Jordan, Lewis, ed. *The New York Times Manual of Style and Usage*. New York: Times Books, 1976.

Lambuth, David. *The Golden Book on Writing*. Collaborators, K.A. Robinson; H.E. Joyce; W.B. Pressey; and A.A. Raven; new chapter by Walter O'Meara. Originally published by Dartmouth College, Hannover, 1923. Reprint. New York: Sullivan, Stauffer, Colwell & Bayles, 1963.

Management Practice: 10th Anniversary. New York: Main, Jackson & Garfield, 1981.

A Manual of Style. 13th ed. Chicago: The University of Chicago Press, 1982.

McKinsey Quarterly, The. Roland Mann, ed. New York: McKinsey & Co. Summer 1980, Autum 1980, Winter 1981, Spring 1981, Autumn 1981, Winter 1982, Spring 1982.

McWilliams, Peter A. *The Word Processing Book: A Short Course in Computer Literacy.* Los Angeles: Prelude Press, 1982.

The Merriam-Webster Handbook of Effective Business Correspondence. New York: Wallaby, 1979.

Miller, Casey, and Swift, Kate. *The Handbook of Nonsexist Writing.* New York: Lippincott & Crowell, 1980.

Miller, Don Ethan. *The Book of Jargon: An Essential Guide to Medicalese, Legalese, Computerese, Basic Jock and 21 Other Varieties of Today's Most Important Specialized Languages.* New York: Macmillan Publishing Co., 1981 (hardcover); Collier Books, 1982 (paperback).

Naczi, Frances D. *Without Bombast and Blunders: An Executive's Guide to Effective Writing.* Rockville Centre, N.Y.: Farnsworth Publishing Co., 1980.

Newman, Edwin. *On Language.* New York: Warner Books, 1980.

The New Yorker. June 21, 1982.

Nystrom, Paul H., ed. *Marketing Handbook.* New York: Ronald Press, 1948.

Onions, C.T., ed. *The Shorter Oxford English Dictionary.* 3rd ed. Oxford: Clarendon Press, 1980.

Paxson, William C. *The Business Writing Handbook: The Essential Guide to Written Communication for People in Business, Government, and the Professions.* New York: Bantam Books, 1981.

Pence, Raymond W. *Style Book in English.* New York: Odyssey Press, 1944.

Posner, Mitchell J. *Executive Essentials.* New York: Avon Books, 1982.

Quinn, Jim. *American Tongue and Cheek: A Populist Guide to Our Language.* New York: Pantheon Books, 1980 (hardcover); Penguin Books, 1982 (paperback).

Rivers, William E. *Business Reports: Samples from the "Real World."* Englewood Cliffs, N.J.: Prentice-Hall, 1981

Roman, Kenneth, and Raphaelson, Joel. *Writing That Works: How to write memos, letters, reports, speeches, resumes, plans, and other papers that say what you mean—and get things done.* New York: Harper & Row, 1981.

Russell, Peter. *The Brain Book.* New York: Dutton, 1984

Safire, William. *On Language.* New York: Times Books, 1980 (hardcover); Avon Books, 1981 (paperback).

Salisbury, Harrison E. *Black Night, White Snow: Russia's Revolutions, 1905–17.* New York: Doubleday Publishing Co., 1978 (hardcover); Da Capo Press, 1981 (paperback).

Schlesinger, Edward S. "English: A Second Language for Lawyers." *One on One: Newsletter of the General Practice Section of the New York State Bar Association.* 3(1982): 6–10.

Shaw, Fran Weber. *30 Ways to Help You Write.* New York: Bantam Books, 1980.

Strunk, William, Jr., and White, E.B. *The Elements of Style.* New York: Macmillan Publishing Co., 1959.

Temple, Michael. *A Pocket Guide to English.* Woodbury: Barron's Educational Series, 1982.

Trueblood, Carol and Fenn, Donna, eds. *The Hazards of Walking: And Other Memos from Your Bureaucrats.* Boston: Houghton Mifflin Co., 1982.

Weiss, Allen. *Write What You Mean: A Handbook of Business Communication.* New York: Amacom, 1977.

Whitman, Digby. "Still More on Quotations: The Home-made Bartlett." *Speechwriter's Newsletter.* November 20, 1981: 2.

Wood, Alden S. "Are you Writing More and Communicating Less?" *BFG Today* (B.F. Goodrich). 4 (1980); 12–13.

————. "Dump Humpty!" *WE* (Western Electric). November–December 1979: 6–7.

————. "The Typochondriac." *The Raglan Report.* November 2, 1981; January 4, 1982; February 1, 1982; April 5, 1982.

The Written Word. Based on The American Heritage Dictionary. Boston: Houghton Mifflin Co., 1977.

Zinsser, William. *On Writing Well.* New York: Harper & Row, 1980 (hardcover); Harper Colophon Books, 1980 (paperback).

Index

134